TEACHER'S PET PUBLICATIONS

LITPLAN TEACHER PACK
for

A Streetcar Named Desire
based on the play by
Tennessee Williams

Written by
Jill Bloomfield

© 2008 Teacher's Pet Publications
All Rights Reserved

Copyright 2008

Only the student materials in this unit plan (such as worksheets, study questions, and tests) may be reproduced multiple times for use in the purchaser's classroom.

For any additional copyright questions, contact Teacher's Pet Publications.

www.tpet.com

TABLE OF CONTENTS - *A Streetcar Named Desire*

Introduction	5
Unit Objectives	8
Reading Assignment Sheet	9
Unit Outline	10
Study Questions (Short Answer)	13
Quiz/Study Questions (Multiple Choice)	24
Pre-reading Vocabulary Worksheets	45
Lesson One (Introductory Lesson)	69
Oral Reading Evaluation Form	71
Writing Assignment 1	75
Writing Evaluation Form	76
Writing Assignment 2	83
Non-fiction Assignment Sheet	85
Extra Writing Assignments/Discussion ?s	95
Writing Assignment 3	97
Vocabulary Review Activities	100
Unit Review Activities	104
Unit Tests	109
Unit Resource Materials	149
Vocabulary Resource Materials	171

A FEW NOTES ABOUT THE AUTHOR TENNESSEE WILLIAMS

Thomas Lanier "Tennessee" Williams is highly regarded as one of the most important American playwrights of the twentieth century. Born in 1911, Williams's life spanned a time of great changes in American culture, as he died in 1983.

Williams had a difficult childhood, as his father was abusive and his mother was extremely controlling. Williams had a brother, Dakin, and a sister, Rose. By the time he was in his teens, Williams was already writing, and he enjoyed it so much that he intended to study it in college. He spent a year at the University of Missouri, and despite his skillfulness as a writer, his father forced him to quit and join him in selling shoes. Deeply disappointed, Williams suffered from depression and eventually a nervous breakdown. Williams's father later relented, and Williams continued his studies at the University of Washington and the University of Iowa, where he eventually earned a degree. Williams continued writing and earned almost immediate renown when his play *The Glass Menagerie* was produced.

Williams's Southern heritage and family life became strong influences on his writing. While Williams was a prolific writer, writing several books of fiction and poetry, he is best known for his plays, which echo his family and personal conflicts and highlight themes including abuse, mental illness, alcoholism, addiction, and homosexuality. A hallmark of Williams's plays is a dark sense of dread and danger. This, and the intensity of his characters and the desperation they feel, is part of a tradition of writing called the Southern Gothic, of which Williams was a master. The Southern Gothic explores the social and cultural aftermath of the institution of slavery, where racism, ignorance, loneliness, dislocation, and loss of power are influences on characters.

Williams's work also often explores the darker side of family life, and again his own life proved to be a deep well from which to draw. His ability to depict the painfully human stories of his characters was widely celebrated, and he won a Pulitzer Prize and a Tony Award during his writing career. Perhaps best known for works such as *A Streetcar Named Desire*, *The Glass Menagerie,* and *Cat on a Hot Tin Roof,* more than a dozen of Williams's plays were adapted to become films.

Tennessee Williams shared a similar malaise of many of his characters. Later in his life, sparked by the death of his lover, he sank into a deep depression, which he fueled by abusing alcohol and prescription drugs. Williams died accidentally when he choked on the cap of a prescription bottle during a binge, unable to escape fate–much like the tragic figures of his plays.

INTRODUCTION

This LitPlan has been designed to develop students' reading, writing, thinking, and language skills through exercises and activities related to *A Streetcar Named Desire*. It includes 21 lessons, supported by extra resource materials.

The **introductory lesson** introduces students to the centrality of relationships and expectations that correspond to them within the play. Following the introductory activity, students are given a transition to explain how the activity relates to the book they are about to read. Following the transition, students are given the materials they will be using during the unit. At the end of the lesson, students begin the pre-reading work for the first reading assignment.

The **reading assignments** are approximately thirty pages each; some are a little shorter while others are a little longer. Students have approximately 15 minutes of pre-reading work to do prior to each reading assignment. This pre-reading work involves reviewing the study questions for the assignment and doing some vocabulary work for 6 to 10 vocabulary words they will encounter in their reading.

The **study guide questions** are fact-based questions; students can find the answers to these questions right in the text. These questions come in two formats: short answer or multiple choice. The best use of these materials is probably to use the short answer version of the questions as study guides for students (since answers will be more complete), and to use the multiple choice version for occasional quizzes.

The **vocabulary work** is intended to enrich students' vocabularies as well as to aid in the students' understanding of the book. Prior to each reading assignment, students will complete a two-part worksheet for approximately 6 to 10 vocabulary words in the upcoming reading assignment. Part I focuses on students' use of general knowledge and contextual clues by giving the sentence in which the word appears in the text. Students are then to write down what they think the words mean based on the words' usage. Part II nails down the definitions of the words by giving students dictionary definitions of the words and having students match the words to the correct definitions based on the words' contextual usage. Students should then have an understanding of the words when they meet them in the text.

After each reading assignment, students will go back and formulate answers for the study guide questions. Discussion of these questions serves as a **review** of the most important events and ideas presented in the reading assignments.

After students complete reading the work, there is a **vocabulary review** lesson which pulls together all of the fragmented vocabulary lists for the reading assignments and gives students a review of all of the words they have studied.

A lesson is devoted to the **extra discussion questions/writing assignments**. These questions focus on interpretation, critical analysis, and personal response, employing a variety of thinking skills and adding to the students' understanding of the novel.

There is an **independent project** in this unit. Students will create time capsules to contain the mementos of their lives, as Blanche has her love letters, tiara and dresses, and they will write about the symbolic importance of each item.

There are three **writing assignments** in this unit, each with the purpose of informing, persuading, or having students express personal opinions. The first assignment gives students an opportunity to use details from the play to write a letter to Stella, advising her on her relationship with Stanley. Though students will adopt a persona from which to write, they should express their personal opinions about Stanley as both a husband and father. The second writing assignment asks students to practice using secondary sources and to write using facts gleaned from them. Students will write a report detailing an actual incident in which someone suffered as a result of discrimination. This assignment will use the articles students prepared for their non-fiction reading assignment. The final writing assignment requires students to write persuasively about connections they perceive between passages. Students will select three passages which they feel "echo" one another in some way. Students must analyze their passages and put forward an argument about the significance of their discovery.

There is a **non-fiction reading assignment**. Students must read non-fiction articles, books, etc. to learn more about discrimination on the basis of race, gender, class, age or sexual orientation.

The **review lesson** pulls together all of the aspects of the unit. The teacher is given four or five choices of activities or games to use which all serve the same basic function of reviewing all of the information presented in the unit.

The **unit test** comes in two formats: multiple choice or short answer. As a convenience, two different tests for each format have been included. There is also an advanced short answer unit test for advanced students.

There are additional **support materials** included with this unit. The **Unit Resource Materials** section includes suggestions for an in-class library, crossword, and word search puzzles related to the novel, and extra worksheets. There is a list of **bulletin board ideas** which gives the teacher suggestions for bulletin boards to go along with this unit. In addition, there is a list of **extra class activities** the teacher could choose from to enhance the unit or as a substitution for an exercise the teacher might feel is inappropriate for his/her class. **Answer keys** are located directly after the **reproducible student materials** throughout the unit. The **Vocabulary Resource Materials** section includes similar worksheets and games to reinforce the vocabulary words.

The **level** of this unit can be varied depending upon the criteria on which the individual assignments are graded, the teacher's expectations of his/her students in class discussions, and the formats chosen for the study guides, quizzes and test. If teachers have other ideas/activities they wish to use, they can usually easily be inserted prior to the review lesson.

The student materials may be reproduced for use in the teacher's classroom without infringement of copyrights. No other portion of this unit may be reproduced without the written consent of Teacher's Pet Publications, Inc.

UNIT OBJECTIVES - *A Streetcar Named Desire*

1. Through reading Tennessee Williams's *A Streetcar Named Desire*, students will study the subtleties of characterization to understand the redemptive qualities of flawed characters.

2. Students will demonstrate their understanding of the text on four levels: factual, interpretive, critical, and personal.

3. Students will explore the importance of motif, paying especial attention to motifs related to the senses.

4. Students will be given the opportunity to practice reading aloud and silently to improve their skills in each area.

5. Students will practice writing fiction, as inspired by the play.

6. Students will consider their attitudes toward aging and will document their adolescence through a scrapbook project.

7. Students will answer questions to demonstrate their knowledge and understanding of the main events and characters in *A Streetcar Named Desire* as they relate to the author's theme development.

8. Students will enrich their vocabularies and improve their understanding of the novel through the vocabulary lessons prepared for use in conjunction with the novel.

9. The writing assignments in this unit are geared to several purposes:
    a. To have students demonstrate their abilities to inform, to persuade, or to express their own personal ideas
        Note: Students will demonstrate the ability to write effectively to <u>inform</u> by developing and organizing facts to convey information. Students will demonstrate the ability to write effectively to <u>persuade</u> by selecting and organizing relevant information, establishing an argumentative purpose, and by designing an appropriate strategy for an identified audience. Students will demonstrate the ability to write effectively to <u>express personal ideas</u> by selecting a form and its appropriate elements.
    b. To check the students' reading comprehension
    c. To make students think about the ideas presented by the novel
    d. To encourage logical thinking
    e. To provide an opportunity to practice good grammar and improve students' use of the English language.

READING ASSIGNMENT SHEET - *A Streetcar Named Desire*

Date Assigned	Scenes Assigned	Completion Date
	1	
	2	
	3	
	4	
	5	
	6	
	7	
	8	
	9	
	10	
	11	

UNIT OUTLINE - *A Streetcar Named Desire*

1 Introduction PVR 1 Oral Reading	2 Study ?s 1 PVR 2 Character Examination	3 Study ?s 2 Writing Assignment #1 PVR 3	4 Study ?s 3 Poker Theme and Motif PVR 4	5 Study ?s 4 Freewrite PVR 5
6 Study ?s 5 Juxatposition PV 6	7 R 6 Study ?s 6 Oral Reading Evaluation PVR 7	8 Study ?s 7 Birthday Art Activity PVR 8	9 Study ?s 8 Writing Assignment #2 Nonfiction Reading PVR 9	10 Non-fiction Reading Library Writing Conferences
11 Study ?s 9 Critical Thinking/Group Work PVR 10	12 Study ?s 10 Symbols PVR 11	13 Study ?s 11 Close Passage Analysis Project	14 Character Improvisation	15 Extra Discussion Questions Writing Assignment #3
16 Complete Writing Assignment #3 Vocabulary Review	17 Fiction Writing Workshop	18 Fiction Writing Workshop	19 Vocabulary Review	20 Test Review
21 Unit Test				

Key: P = Preview Study Questions V = Vocabulary Work R= Read

STUDY GUIDE QUESTIONS

SHORT ANSWER STUDY GUIDE QUESTIONS - *A Streetcar Named Desire*

Scene 1
1. In what city is the play set?
2. What does Stanley carry as he enters at the beginning of the play?
3. To what does Williams compare Blanche's manner and clothing in the stage directions?
4. What directions was Blanche given to Stella's place?
5. What relationship is Blanche to Stella?
6. What job did Blanche previously have?
7. What is Belle Reve?
8. How does Blanche feel about Stella's home?
9. Why does Blanche say she left her job?
10. What happened to Belle Reve?

Scene 2
1. What about herself does Stella ask Stanley not to mention to Blanche?
2. What, according to Stella, is Blanche's "little weakness"?
3. What does Stanley say the Napoleonic Code is?
4. What favor does Blanche ask Stanley?
5. Why does Blanche ask Stella to get her a Coke at the drugstore?
6. What does Blanche say she'll burn?
7. For what does Stella apologize to Blanche?
8. Why do Blanche and Stella go out on poker night?

Scene 3
1. Why doesn't Mitch enjoy going out?
2. Describe the joke Steve tells.
3. What about Stanley makes Stella think that he will succeed in life?
4. Who gave Mitch his silver cigarette case?
5. What does the name Blanche mean?
6. What does the name DuBois mean?
7. What lies does Blanche tell Mitch about Stella?
8. After Blanche and Mitch begin dancing, what does Stanley do with the radio?
9. For what does Blanche thank Mitch?

Streetcar Named Desire Short Answer Study Questions Page 2

Scene 4
1. What did Stanley do on his and Stella's wedding night?
2. What was Stella's response to Stanley's wedding night behavior?
3. What does Stella mean when she says she is not in anything that she has a desire to get out of?
4. Who is Shep Huntleigh?
5. How much money does Blanche have?
6. Blanche tells Stella she can't live with Stanley. Why can't she?
7. What does Blanche say about Stanley when she speaks "plainly" about him?
8. Of what are Blanche and Stella unaware as Blanche speaks "plainly" about Stanley?

Scene 5
1. Of what does Eunice accuse Steve?
2. To where does Eunice go after her fight with Steve?
3. Why does Blanche think Stanley is an Aries?
4. What astrological sign is Blanche?
5. Who is Shaw?
6. How does Blanche respond physically (according to the stage directions) to Stanley's inquiry about Shaw?
7. What does Blanche say about the Flamingo hotel?
8. What does Blanche say about "soft people"?
9. What does Blanche do when the Coke spills over onto her pretty white skirt?
10. Why does Blanche want to deceive Mitch?
11. Why does Blanche want Mitch?
12. What does Blanche do to the newspaper boy?

Scene 6
1. How does Blanche define "the law of nature"?
2. What does Blanche look for in the sky?
3. What personal information does Mitch ask Blanche while Stanley and Stella are out?
4. Why does Blanche secretly roll her eyes?
5. What does Blanche tell Mitch about Stanley?
6. What does Blanche reveal about her husband?
7. How did Blanche's husband die?

Streetcar Named Desire Short Answer Study Questions Page 3

Scene 7
1. For what occasion is Stella preparing at the opening of Scene Seven?
2. Why did Blanche leave the Flamingo?
3. How does Stella react to Stanley's revelations about Blanche?
4. What song does Blanche sing in the bathtub while Stanley tells Stella what he has learned about Blanche?
5. According to Stanley, why did Blanche leave the school?
6. Why doesn't Mitch come over for the birthday celebration?
7. What did Stella hope about Mitch and Blanche?
8. How does Stanley make sure that Blanche will leave?

Scene 8
1. Describe the funny story (joke) Blanche tells.
2. Why does Stanley hurl a plate to the floor?
3. To whom does "pair of queens" refer?
4. What does Stanley mean by "get the colored lights going"?
5. What does Blanche realize that she shouldn't have done?
6. What does Stanley give Blanche as a birthday present?
7. What does Stella request at the end of Scene Eight?

Scene 9
1. Why does Mitch ask Blanche if she is out of her mind?
2. Why does Mitch turn on the light?
3. How does Blanche respond when Mitch confronts her about the Flamingo?
4. Describe the Mexican woman.
5. What does Blanche say is the opposite of Death?
6. Why doesn't Mitch want to marry Blanche anymore?
7. Why does Blanche scream "Fire! Fire! Fire!"?

Scene 10
1. At the beginning of Scene Ten, what is Blanche wearing?
2. Why did Stanley come home from the hospital?
3. From whom does Blanche claim she has received a telegram?
4. Into what garments does Stanley change when he comes home from the hospital?
5. What will make Blanche "weep with joy"?
6. What lie does Blanche tell Stanley about her meeting with Mitch?
7. What can the audience see through the back wall after Blanche's frantic attempt to call Shep Huntleigh?
8. With what does Blanche physically threaten Stanley?
9. What happens at the end of Scene Ten?

Streetcar Named Desire Short Answer Study Questions Page 4

<u>Scene 11</u>
1. As the final scene opens, what are the men doing?
2. Where is Stella sending Blanche in the final scene of the play?
3. Where does Blanche believe that she is going in the final scene?
4. What advice does Eunice give Stella?
5. What does Blanche say will cause her to die?
6. What item does Stanley ask Blanche if she wants to take with her?
7. On what does Blanche say she has always depended?

ANSWER KEY SHORT ANSWER STUDY GUIDE QUESTIONS
A Streetcar Named Desire

Scene 1
1. In what city is the play set?
   The play is set in New Orleans.

2. What does Stanley carry as he enters at the beginning of the play?
   He carries a bowling jacket and package from the butcher.

3. To what does Williams compare Blanche's manner and clothing in the stage directions?
   Williams compares Blanche to a moth.

4. What directions was Blanche given to Stella's place?
   She was told to take a street-car named Desire, then transfer to one called Cemeteries, and ride six blocks and get off at Elysian Fields.

5. What relationship is Blanche to Stella?
   Blanche is Stella's older sister.

6. What job did Blanche previously have?
   Blanche says she was an English teacher.

7. What is Belle Reve?
   Belle Reve was the DuBois family home/plantation.

8. How does Blanche feel about Stella's home?
   She says only Edgar Allan Poe could do it justice, and she asks why Stella never told her that she has to live in "these conditions."

9. Why does Blanche say she left her job?
   She says her nerves broke.

10. What happened to Belle Reve?
    It was repossessed by the bank.

Scene 2
1. What about herself does Stella ask Stanley not to mention to Blanche?
   Stella asked Stanley not to tell Blanche about her pregnancy.

2. What, according to Stella, is Blanche's "little weakness"?
   Blanche's vanity, her concern over her appearance, is her weakness.

3. What does Stanley say the Napoleonic Code is?
   He says it is spousal ownership of property.

4. What favor does Blanche ask Stanley?
   Blanche asks Stanley to fasten the buttons on her dress.

5. Why does Blanche ask Stella to get her a Coke at the drugstore?
   She wants Stella out of the apartment so she can speak to Stanley candidly.

6. What does Blanche say she'll burn?
   She says she will burn love letters that Stanley has touched.

7. For what does Stella apologize to Blanche?
   She apologizes for Stanley's rudeness.

8. Why do Blanche and Stella go out on poker night?
   They are not invited when the men are playing poker.

Scene 3

1. Why doesn't Mitch enjoy going out?
   He worries about his mother.

2. Describe the joke Steve tells.
   A rooster stops pursuing a hen because a farmer throws corn out to eat.

3. What about Stanley makes Stella think that he will succeed in life?
   Stella says, "It's a drive that he has."

4. Who gave Mitch his silver cigarette case?
   A former girlfriend who is now deceased gave it to him.

5. What does the name Blanche mean?
   Blanche means "white."

6. What does the name DuBois mean?
   DuBois means "wood."

7. What lies does Blanche tell Mitch about Stella?
   Blanche tells Mitch that Stella is older than she is by less than a year and that she has come to help Stella for a while because Stella is very run down.

8. After Blanche and Mitch begin dancing, what does Stanley do with the radio?
   He throws it out the window.

9. For what does Blanche thank Mitch?
   Blanche says, "Thank you for being so kind. I need kindness now."

Scene 4
1. What did Stanley do on his and Stella's wedding night?
   He smashed lightbulbs.

2. What was Stella's response to Stanley's wedding night behavior?
   She was excited by it.

3. What does Stella mean when she says she is not in anything that she has a desire to get out of?
   She is satisfied by her marriage.

4. Who is Shep Huntleigh?
   Shep is Blanche's old beau.

5. How much money does Blanche have?
   She only has 65 cents.

6. Blanche tells Stella she can't live with Stanley. Why can't she?
   She says the only way to live with a man like Stanley is to go to bed with him, and she knows that's Stella's place, not hers.

7. What does Blanche say about Stanley when she speaks "plainly" about him?
   She calls him bestial, animal-like, and ape-like.

8. Of what are Blanche and Stella unaware as Blanche speaks "plainly" about Stanley?
   They are unaware that Stanley is listening to their conversation.

Scene 5
1. Of what does Eunice accuse Steve?
   She accuses him of having an affair with a blonde woman.

2. To where does Eunice go after her fight with Steve?
   She goes to the Four Deuce.

3. Why does Blanche think Stanley is an Aries?
   He bangs inanimate objects around.

4. What astrological sign is Blanche?
    She is a Virgo.

5. Who is Shaw?
    He is Stanley's acquaintance who believes he knows Blanche.

6. How does Blanche respond physically (according to the stage directions) to Stanley's inquiry about Shaw?
    She becomes weak, trembling, fearful, and panicky.

7. What does Blanche say about the Flamingo hotel?
    "The Flamingo Hotel is not the sort of establishment I would dare to be seen in!"

8. What does Blanche say about "soft people"?
    She says "soft people have to shimmer and glow. . . . It isn't enough to be soft. You've got to be soft and attractive."

9. What does Blanche do when the Coke spills over onto her pretty white skirt?
    She gives a piercing cry; she screams.

10. Why does Blanche want to deceive Mitch?
    She wants to deceive him enough to make him want her.

11. Why does Blanche want Mitch?
    She wants him so she can rest, so she can leave Stella's house and not be a problem.

12. What does Blanche do to the newspaper boy?
    She flirts with him, kisses him without his permission, and sends him on his way.

Scene 6

1. How does Blanche define "the law of nature"?
    She says the lady must entertain the gentleman.

2. What does Blanche look for in the sky?
    She looks for the Pleiades/Seven Sisters constellation.

3. What personal information does Mitch ask Blanche while Stanley and Stella are out?
    He asks her age and her weight.

4. Why does Blanche secretly roll her eyes?
    She is amused because she is lying and it is working.

5. What does Blanche tell Mitch about Stanley?
    She says Stanley hates her and is very rude to her.

6. What does Blanche reveal about her husband?
    He was homosexual.

7. How did Blanche's husband die?
    He committed suicide.

Scene 7

1. For what occasion is Stella preparing at the opening of Scene Seven?
    She is preparing for Blanche's birthday.

2. Why did Blanche leave the Flamingo?
    She was asked to leave by management.

3. How does Stella react to Stanley's revelations about Blanche?
    Stella says its all lies.

4. What song does Blanche sing in the bathtub while Stanley tells Stella what he has learned about Blanche?
    She sings *Paper Moon*: "It wouldn't be make-believe if you believed in me!"

5. According to Stanley, why did Blanche leave the school?
    She had gotten "mixed-up with" a seventeen-year-old boy and lost her job.

6. Why doesn't Mitch come over for the birthday celebration?
    Stanley told Mitch about Blanche's past.

7. What did Stella hope about Mitch and Blanche?
    She hoped they would marry.

8. How does Stanley make sure that Blanche will leave?
    He buys her a bus ticket.

Scene 8

1. Describe the funny story (joke) Blanche tells.
    She tells a story about a parrot, an old maid, and a preacher.

2. Why does Stanley hurl a plate to the floor?
    Stella has criticized him, calling him "pig" and "greasy."

3. To whom does "pair of queens" refer?
    It refers to Stella and Blanche.

4. What does Stanley mean by "get the colored lights going"?
    He is talking about engaging in sexual activity with his wife.

5. What does Blanche realize that she shouldn't have done?
   She says she shouldn't have called Mitch.

6. What does Stanley give Blanche as a birthday present?
   He gives Blanche a bus ticket.

7. What does Stella request at the end of Scene Eight?
   She asks to be taken to the hospital.

Scene 9
1. Why does Mitch ask Blanche if she is out of her mind?
   Blanche is talking about music that isn't playing and "the shot." She is somehow re-living the evening her husband killed himself.

2. Why does Mitch turn on the light?
   He wants to look at Blanche in the light to see who she really is.

3. How does Blanche respond when Mitch confronts her about the Flamingo?
   She denies staying there, saying she stayed at the Tarantula Arms Hotel. But then she continues to confess and tell the truth to Mitch.

4. Describe the Mexican woman.
   She is a blind woman in a dark shawl, selling flowers for the dead.

5. What does Blanche say is the opposite of Death?
   Blanche says the opposite of death is desire.

6. Why doesn't Mitch want to marry Blanche anymore?
   She is not clean enough.

7. Why does Blanche scream "Fire! Fire! Fire!"?
   She is trying to make Mitch leave.

Scene 10
1. At the beginning of Scene Ten, what is Blanche wearing?
   She wears a white evening gown, slippers, and a tiara.

2. Why did Stanley come home from the hospital?
   They told him to come home and sleep some since the baby wouldn't come before morning.

3. From whom does Blanche claim she has received a telegram?
   She claims to have received a telegram from Shep Huntleigh.

4. Into what garments does Stanley change when he comes home from the hospital?
    He changes into the silk pajamas from his wedding night.

5. What will make Blanche "weep with joy"?
    She says leaving Stanley and Stella's house and having privacy again will make her "weep with joy."

6. What lie does Blanche tell Stanley about her meeting with Mitch?
    She tells Stanley that Mitch brought her flowers and begged for her forgiveness.

7. What can the audience see through the back wall after Blanche's frantic attempt to call Shep Huntleigh?
    A prostitute has rolled a drunkard. He pursues her along the wall, overtakes her, and there is a struggle. A policeman's whistle breaks it up.

8. With what does Blanche physically threaten Stanley?
    Blanche threatens Stanley with a broken bottle.

9. What happens at the end of Scene Ten?
    Stanley rapes Blanche.

Scene 11
1. As the final scene opens, what are the men doing?
    They are playing poker.

2. Where is Stella sending Blanche in the final scene of the play?
    Stella is sending Blanche to an asylum.

3. Where does Blanche believe that she is going in the final scene?
    She thinks she is going to travel with Shep Huntleigh.

4. What advice does Eunice give Stella?
    "Life has to go on. No matter what happens, you have to keep on going."

5. What does Blanche say will cause her to die?
    She says she will die from eating unwashed grapes.

6. What item does Stanley ask Blanche if she wants to take with her?
    He asks her if she wants to take her paper lantern.

7. On what does Blanche say she has always depended?
    Blanche says she has always depended on the kindness of strangers.

STUDY GUIDE/QUIZ QUESTIONS - *A Streetcar Named Desire*
Multiple Choice Format

<u>Scene 1</u>

1. In what city is the play set?
    A. New York
    B. San Francisco
    C. Milwaukee
    D. New Orleans

2. What does Stanley carry as he enters at the beginning of the play?
    A. Hard hat and a lunch box
    B. Bowling jacket and a package from the butcher
    C. Car keys and a winter coat
    D. Bouquet of flowers and a shopping bag

3. To what does Williams compare Blanche's manner and clothing in the stage directions?
    A. A moth
    B. A hummingbird
    C. A cat
    D. A butterfly

4. What directions was Blanche given to Stella's place?
    A. Take the Blue Line to Love Canal, then the street-car named Desire to the Four Deuces. It's a short walk from there.
    B. Take a street-car named Desire, then transfer to one called Cemeteries. Ride six blocks and get off at Elysian Fields.
    C. Take the street-car named Cemeteries, then transfer to one called Desire. Get off at the Four Deuces; it's a short walk across the Elysian Fields.
    D. Take the street-car from Elysian Fields to one called Desire at the cemetery. Ride Desire to your destination.

5. What relationship is Blanche to Stella?
    A. Younger sister
    B. Step-sister
    C. Older sister
    D. Sorority sister

6. What job did Blanche previously have?
    A. Social worker
    B. Secretary
    C. Teacher
    D. Prostitute

Streetcar Multiple Choice Page 2

7. What is Belle Reve?
    A. DuBois family home
    B. Stella's cousin
    C. A department store
    D. Blanche's perfume

8. How does Blanche feel about Stella's home?
    A. She thinks it is lovely.
    B. She says it is nice, but does not actually mean it.
    C. She says she imagined it would be this cute from Stella's letters.
    D. She says only Edgar Allan Poe could describe "these conditions."

9. Why does Blanche say she left her job?
    A. Her nerves broke.
    B. She was fired.
    C. She was bored.
    D. Her patience was exhausted.

10. What happened to Belle Reve?
    A. It was destroyed by fire.
    B. It is repossessed by the bank.
    C. It was sold by Blanche.
    D. It was spilled.

Streetcar Multiple Choice Page 3

Scene 2
1. What about herself does Stella ask Stanley not to mention to Blanche?
    A. Her pregnancy
    B. Her doubt in Blanche's story
    C. That she actually dislikes Blanche
    D. That she is not actually married

2. What, according to Stella, is Blanche's weakness?
    A. Her concern over her appearance
    B. Her intelligence
    C. Her lack of a husband
    D. Her need for attention

3. What does Stanley say the Napoleonic Code is?
    A. Spousal ownership of property
    B. Conquering territory in France
    C. Husbands own all property
    D. Unconditional honesty

4. What favor does Blanche ask Stanley?
    A. To borrow $20
    B. To ask Mitch on a date for her
    C. To fasten the buttons on her dress
    D. To teach her how to play poker

5. Why does Blanche ask Stella to get her a Coke at the drugstore?
    A. Because she is thirsty
    B. Because she likes to control Stella
    C. So she can kiss Stanley
    D. So she can speak to Stanley candidly

6. What does Blanche say she'll burn?
    A. The deed to Belle Reve
    B. Love letters that Stanley has touched
    C. The dress she traveled in
    D. A book of poems

7. For what does Stella apologize to Blanche?
    A. For not getting a Coke
    B. For Stanley's rudeness
    C. For never writing letters
    D. For having such a small home

Streetcar Multiple Choice Page 4

8. Why do Blanche and Stella go out on poker night?
    A. Because they want to celebrate Stella's pregnancy
    B. Because they need to buy groceries
    C. Because they want to visit the graveyard
    D. Because they are not invited to play poker

Streetcar Multiple Choice Page 5

Scene 3
1. Why doesn't Mitch enjoy going out?
    A. He has too much work to do.
    B. He worries about his mother.
    C. He is too shy.
    D. He does not have enough money.

2. Describe the joke Steve tells.
    A. Two monkeys have a conversation about life.
    B. Women and men speak different languages.
    C. A farmer sees a spaceship in the sky.
    D. A rooster stops pursuing a hen because a farmer throws corn out to eat.

3. What about Stanley makes Stella think that he will succeed in life?
    A. His ability to save money
    B. His drive
    C. His deep dedication to their happiness
    D. His desire to be a father

4. Who gave Mitch his silver cigarette case?
    A. His mother
    B. Stella
    C. Stanley
    D. A former girlfriend

5. What does the name Blanche mean?
    A. White
    B. Sweet
    C. Lily
    D. Beauty

6. What does the name DuBois mean?
    A. Two petals
    B. Wood
    C. Willow tree
    D. Rose

7. What lie does Blanche tell Mitch about Stella?
    A. That she is having a baby
    B. That Stella was married before Stanley
    C. That she is older than Blanche
    D. That she is planning to leave Stanley

Streetcar Multiple Choice Page 6

8. After Blanche and Mitch begin dancing, what does Stanley do with the radio?
    A. Turns it to another station
    B. Sings along with it
    C. Punches it
    D. Throws it out the window

9. For what does Blanche thank Mitch?
    A. A bouquet of carnations
    B. A bottle of wine
    C. Kindness
    D. Money he loaned her

Streetcar Multiple Choice Page 7

Scene 4
1. What did Stanley do on his and Stella's wedding night?
    A. Smashed lightbulbs
    B. Carried Stella over the threshold
    C. Gave Stella a poem
    D. Went bowling

2. What was Stella's response to Stanley's wedding night behavior?
    A. Happiness
    B. Anger
    C. Disdain
    D. Excitement

3. What does Stella mean when she says she is not in anything that she has a desire to get out of?
    A. She wants Blanche to live with them forever.
    B. She wants to reunite with Shep.
    C. She is satisfied by her marriage.
    D. She wants her affair with Mitch to remain secret.

4. Who is Shep Huntleigh?
    A. Blanche's old beau
    B. Stanley's bowling buddy
    C. Stella's old beau
    D. A relative of Blanche and Stella

5. How much money does Blanche have?
    A. Blanche has no money.
    B. Blanche has 65 cents.
    C. Blanche has $100,000.00 left from the sale of Belle Reve.
    D. Blanche has $19.75.

6. How does Blanche say is the only way to "live with such a man" as Stanley?
    A. Ignore him
    B. Keep him sober
    C. Pretend the situation is fine
    D. Go to bed with him

7. What does Blanche say about Stanley when she speaks "plainly" about him?
    A. He is bestial, animal-like, and ape-like.
    B. He is lazy and rude, and he stinks.
    C. He is attractive but vulgar.
    D. He is too concerned with poker and doesn't pay enough attention to Stella.

Streetcar Multiple Choice Page 8

8. Of what are Blanche and Stella unaware as Blanche speaks "plainly" about Stanley?
   A. Mitch is listening to their conversation.
   B. The Four Deuces is on fire.
   C. Stanley is listening to their conversation.
   D. Shep Huntleigh has arrived.

Streetcar Multiple Choice Page 9

Scene 5
1. Of what does Eunice accuse Steve?
    A. Having an affair with a blonde woman
    B. Cheating at poker
    C. Cheating at bowling
    D. Spending their money recklessly

2. To where does Eunice go after her fight with Steve?
    A. To Stella's apartment
    B. To ride the streetcar
    C. To buy a Coke
    D. To the Four Deuces

3. Why does Blanche think Stanley is an Aries?
    A. Because he is sensitive
    B. Because he bangs inanimate objects around
    C. Because he has thick hair
    D. Because he is stubborn

4. What astrological sign is Blanche?
    A. Leo
    B. Virgo
    C. Taurus
    D. Capricorn

5. Who is Shaw?
    A. Blanche's old beau
    B. Shep's cousin
    C. Stanley's acquaintance
    D. Drugstore clerk

6. How does Blanche respond physically (according to the stage directions) to Stanley's inquiry about Shaw?
    A. She becomes weak, trembling, fearful and panicky.
    B. She becomes happy and jubilant.
    C. She becomes overwhelmed with anger.
    D. She giggles uncontrollably.

Streetcar Multiple Choice Page 10

7. What does Blanche say about the Flamingo Hotel?
    A. It was the most exciting place in town.
    B. It was where all the men went to play poker.
    C. It was the kind of a place she wouldn't dare to be seen in.
    D. It was her favorite place to go for dinner.

8. What does Blanche say about "soft people"?
    A. They make her sick.
    B. They are the most sensitive, the most caring, and the most loving people.
    C. They have to shimmer and glow.
    D. They ride a street-car named Desire.

9. What does Blanche do when the Coke spills over onto her pretty white skirt?
    A. She screams.
    B. She laughs.
    C. She slaps Mitch.
    D. She cries.

10. Why does Blanche want to deceive Mitch?
    A. She is just toying with him.
    B. She thinks he deserves it.
    C. She can't bring herself to tell him the truth.
    D. She wants him to want her.

11. Why does Blanche want Mitch?
    A. She wants him so she can rest and leave Stella's house.
    B. She wants to make Stanley jealous.
    C. She wants to make Stella jealous.
    D. She wants to prove to Shep she is still desirable to other men.

12. Describe Blanche's interaction with the newspaper boy.
    A. First she aks him to forget the bill, then she cries because she is poor.
    B. First she invites him in for a drink, then she kisses him without his permission.
    C. First she invites him in for milk, then she give him freshly baked cookies.
    D. First he flirts with her, then he kisses her without her permission.

Streetcar Multiple Choice Page 11

Scene 6
1. How does Blanche define "the law of nature"?
    A. She says the lady must entertain the gentleman.
    B. She says the weak always lose.
    C. She says problems always work out.
    D. She says men must protect women.

2. What does Blanche look for in the sky?
    A. A shooting star
    B. The Pleiades
    C. The moon
    D. An airplane

3. What personal information does Mitch ask Blanche while Stella and Stanley are out?
    A. What happened to her husband
    B. Why she is so soft
    C. Her age and weight
    D. Whether or not she had any children

4. Why does Blanche secretly roll her eyes?
    A. She thinks of Stanley.
    B. She is bored.
    C. She is amused because she is lying and it is working.
    D. She thinks she is better than everyone else.

5. What does Blanche tell Mitch about Stanley?
    A. Stanley hates her and is rude.
    B. Stanley desires her.
    C. Stanley lies.
    D. She is uncontrollably attracted to Stanley.

6. What does Blanche reveal about her husband?
    A. She killed him.
    B. He was homosexual.
    C. She never loved him.
    D. He asked her for a divorce.

7. How did Blanche's husband die?
    A. Murder
    B. Drowning
    C. Heart failure
    D. Suicide

Streetcar Multiple Choice Page 12

Scene 7

1. For what occasion is Stella preparing at the opening of Scene Seven?
    A. Stanley's birthday
    B. Eunice's birthday
    C. Steve's birthday
    D. Blanche's birthday

2. Why did Blanche leave the Flamingo?
    A. She was fired.
    B. She was bored with it.
    C. She was never there in the first place.
    D. She was asked to leave by management.

3. How does Stella react to Stanley's revelations about Blanche?
    A. She thanks him.
    B. She says its all lies.
    C. She said she already knew all that he told her.
    D. She thinks he is jealous of Blanche.

4. What song does Blanche sing in the bathtub while Stanley tells Stella what he has learned about Blanche?
    A. She is singing *Happy Days Are Here Again:* "Your cares and troubles are gone, there'll be no more from now on."
    B. She is singing *Paper Moon:* "It wouldn't be make-believe if you believed in me!"
    C. She is singing *Auld Lang Syne:* "Should old acquaintance be forgot, and never brought to mind?"
    D. She is singing *Amazing Grace:* "I once was lost, but now am found."

5. According to Stanley, why did Blanche leave the school?
    A. She had told the truth about her nerves and quite to get some rest.
    B. She had gotten "mixed-up with" a seventeen-year-old boy and lost her job.
    C. She had been offered a better position at another school.
    D. She had gotten "mixed-up with" a married man and lost her job.

6. Why doesn't Mitch come over for the birthday celebration?
    A. He has to work late.
    B. His mother is ill.
    C. Stanley told Mitch about Blanche's past.
    D. He has to go to church.

Streetcar Multiple Choice Page 13

7. What did Stella hope about Mitch and Blanche?
    A. She hoped they would marry.
    B. She hoped they would go away.
    C. She hoped they would be godparents.
    D. She hoped they would dance.

8. How does Stanley make sure that Blanche will leave?
    A. He buys her a bus ticket.
    B. He packs her suitcase.
    C. He forbids her to use the bathroom.
    D. He kicks Stella out.

Streetcar Multiple Choice Page 14

Scene 8

1. Describe the funny story (joke) Blanche tells.
    A. She tells a story about when she became prom queen.
    B. She tells a story about a parrot, an old maid, and a preacher.
    C. She tells a story about a boy who told lies.
    D. She tells a story about a puppy who loses his way.

2. Why does Stanley hurl a plate to the floor?
    A. His food tasted unpleasant.
    B. No one paid any attention to him.
    C. Stella has criticized him, calling him a "pig" and "greasy."
    D. Blanche has criticized him, calling him a "pig" and "greasy."

3. To whom does "pair of queens" refer?
    A. It refers to the queen of hearts and queen of diamonds in a deck of cards.
    B. If refers to the bar tenders at the Four Deuces.
    C. It refers to Stella and Blanche.
    D. It refers to Stella's mother and Blanche.

4. What does Stanley mean by "get the colored lights going"?
    A. Engage in sexual activity with his wife
    B. Decorate their apartment
    C. Become enraged
    D. Have an argument

5. What does Blanche realize that she shouldn't have done?
    A. Hit Stanley
    B. Threatened Stella
    C. Seduced Mitch
    D. Called Mitch

6. What does Stanley give Blanche as a birthday present?
    A. A suitcase
    B. A bus ticket
    C. An antique tiara
    D. A check for $100

7. What does Stella request at the end of Scene Eight?
    A. To have everyone get along
    B. To be taken to the hospital
    C. To go to the bowling alley
    D. To drink a coke

Streetcar Multiple Choice Page 15

Scene 9

1. Why does Mitch ask Blanche if she is out of her mind?
    A. Because she is talking to his mother
    B. Because she is pulling out her hair
    C. Because she can hear music that is not actually playing
    D. Because she is crying hysterically

2. Why does Mitch turn on the light?
    A. To see Blanche better
    B. Blanche is afraid of the dark
    C. The movie is over
    D. The sun has set

3. How does Blanche respond when Mitch confronts her about the Flamingo?
    A. At first she denies being there.
    B. She bursts into (fake) tears feigning insult.
    C. Blanche asks where on earth he heard such a silly thing.
    D. She faints.

4. Describe the Mexican woman and tell what she does.
    A. She is a beautiful woman with dark hair; she nods knowingly at Blanche.
    B. She is colorfully dressed and sells handmade blankets.
    C. She is blind and sells flowers for the dead.
    D. She is frightful-looking and tries to rob and strangle Blanche.

5. What does Blanche say is the opposite of Death?
    A. Life
    B. Desire
    C. Truth
    D. Innocence

6. Why doesn't Mitch want to marry Blanche anymore?
    A. He says she is not clean enough.
    B. He thinks she is too young.
    C. He thinks she is too old.
    D. His old girlfriend has come back to him.

8. Why does Blanche scream, "Fire! Fire! Fire!"
    A. The building next door is on fire.
    B. Stanley is trying to rape her, and she needs help.
    C. Stanley has gone into a rage.
    D. She wants Mitch to leave.

Streetcar Multiple Choice Page 16

Scene 10

1. At the beginning of Scene Ten, what is Blanche wearing?
    A. White bathrobe
    B. White evening gown, slippers, tiara
    C. Stanley's bowling shirt
    D. An apron

2. Why did Stanley come home from the hospital?
    A. They told him the baby wouldn't come until morning.
    B. Stella died.
    C. He couldn't take the pressure of being there.
    D. He wanted Blanche.

3. From whom does Blanche claim she has received a telegram?
    A. Belle Reve
    B. Bill Shaw
    C. The manager of The Flamingo
    D. Shep Huntleigh

4. Into what garments does Stanley change when he comes home from the hospital?
    A. His bowling shirt
    B. Jeans and a white t-shirt
    C. Silk pajamas from his wedding night
    D. Slacks and a dressy shirt

5. What will make Blanche "weep with joy"?
    A. Reuniting with Shep
    B. Leaving Stella and Stanley–and having privacy again
    C. Having a niece or nephew
    D. Being told she is beautiful

6. What lie does Blanche tell Stanley about her meeting with Mitch?
    A. That he brought her flowers and begged for her forgiveness
    B. That he proposed
    C. That Mitch attempted to rape her
    D. That she told Mitch how much she loves him

7. Which figures appear in the shadows of the back wall?
    A. A prostitute, a drunk, a policeman
    B. Angel, Blanche's mother, Stella, Stanley
    C. Mitch, Mitch's mother, a bride and groom
    D. Stanley, Stella, Steve, and Eunice

Streetcar Multiple Choice Page 17

8. With what does Blanche physically threaten Stanley?
    A. A Gun
    B. A knife
    C. A broken bottle
    D. Shards of a mirror

9. What happens at the end of Scene Ten?
    A. Stella has her baby.
    B. Stanley rapes Blanche.
    C. Blanche steals a kiss from Stanley.
    D. Blanche runs away.

Streetcar Multiple Choice Page 18

Scene 11

1. As the final scene opens, what are the men doing?
    A. Painting the apartment
    B. Carrying groceries
    C. Taunting the women
    D. Playing poker

2. Where is Stella sending Blanche in the final scene?
    A. On a vacation to Miami
    B. Aunt Ethel's house
    C. An asylum
    D. Belle Reve

3. Where does Blanche believe that she is going at the end of the play?
    A. To travel with Shep Huntleigh
    B. To the Four Deuces
    C. To ride on a train
    D. To Belle Reve

4. What advice does Eunice give Stella?
    A. Divorce Stanley and move away with the baby
    B. No matter what happens, you have to keep on going
    C. Disown Blanche entirely
    D. Follow your own street-car named Desire

5. What does Blanche say will cause her to die?
    A. Unrequited love
    B. Guilt
    C. Eating unwashed grapes
    D. Heart failure

6. What item does Stanley ask Blanche if she wants to take with her?
    A. Her bathrobe
    B. Her paper lantern
    C. A bottle of gin
    D. A photo of the baby

7. On what does Blanche say she has always depended?
    A. The kindness of strangers
    B. Her stunning good looks
    C. Her ability to seduce
    D. Her good reputation

ANSWER KEY - MULTIPLE CHOICE STUDY/QUIZ QUESTIONS
A Streetcar Named Desire

	1	2	3	4	5	6	7	8	9	10	11
1	D	A	B	A	A	A	D	B	C	B	D
2	B	A	D	D	D	B	D	C	A	A	C
3	A	A	B	C	B	C	B	C	A	D	A
4	B	C	D	A	B	C	B	A	C	C	B
5	C	D	A	B	C	A	B	D	B	B	C
6	C	B	B	D	A	B	C	B	A	A	B
7	A	B	C	A	C	D	A	B	D	A	A
8	D	D	D	C	C		A			C	
9	A		C		A					B	
10	B				D						
11					A						
12					B						
13											

PREREADING VOCABULARY WORKSHEETS

VOCABULARY - *A Streetcar Named Desire*

Scene 1 Part I: Using Prior Knowledge and Contextual Clues

Below are the sentences in which the vocabulary words appear in the text. Read the sentence. Use any clues you can find in the sentence combined with your prior knowledge, and write what you think the underlined words mean on the lines provided.

1. The section is poor, but unlike other American cities, it has a raffish charm.

_____

2. You can almost feel the warm breath of the brown river beyond the river warehouses with their faint redolences of bananas and coffee.

_____

3. . . . for New Orleans is a cosmopolitan city where there is a relatively warm and easy intermingling of races in the old part of town.

_____

4. Blanche comes around the corner carrying a valise.

_____

5. Her appearance is incongruous to this setting.

_____

6. She begins to speak with feverish vivacity. . . .

_____

7. They're a mixed lot . . . Heterogeneous—types?

_____

8. Well, Stella–you're going to reproach me, I know that you're bound to reproach me. . . .

_____

A Streetcar Named Desire Vocabulary Worksheet Scene 1 Continued

9. He holds the bottle to the light to observe its <u>depletion</u>.

_____

10. I'm afraid I'll strike you as being the <u>unrefined</u> type.

_____

Part II: Determining the Meaning
　Match the vocabulary words to their dictionary definitions.

｜　　1. raffish　　　　　　A. crude; unpolished
｜　　2. redolences　　　　 B. blame
｜　　3. cosmopolitan　　　 C. liveliness
｜　　4. valise　　　　　　 D. scarcity
｜　　5. incongruous　　　　E. different
｜　　6. vivacity　　　　　 F. odors; fragrances
｜　　7. heterogeneous　　　G. out of place
｜　　8. reproach　　　　　 H. worldly
｜　　9. depletion　　　　　I. vulgar
｜　　10. unrefined　　　　 J. suitcase

VOCABULARY - *A Streetcar Named Desire*

Scene 2 Part I: Using Prior Knowledge and Contextual Clues

Below are the sentences in which the vocabulary words appear in the text. Read the sentence. Use any clues you can find in the sentence combined with your prior knowledge, and write what you think the underlined words mean on the lines provided.

1. Stanley enters the kitchen from outside, leaving the door open on the perpetual "blue piano" around the corner.

_____

2. Stanley [ominously]: So?

_____

3. Now lets's have a gander at the bill of sale.

_____

4. She didn't show you no paper, no deed of sale or nothing like that, huh?

_____

5. . . . anyone of our family could have perpetrated a swindle on anyone else.

_____

6. . . . anyone of our family could have perpetrated a swindle on anyone else.

_____

7. You're simple, straightforward and honest, and a little bit on the primitive side. . . .

_____

8. These are love letters, yellowing with antiquity. . . .

_____

9. . . . our improvident grandfathers and father and uncles and brothers exchanged the land for their epic fornications–to put it plainly.

_____

A Streetcar Named Desire Vocabulary Worksheet Scene 2 Continued

10. . . . our improvident grandfathers and father and uncles and brothers exchanged the land for their epic <u>fornications</u>–to put it plainly.

_____

Part II: Determining the Meaning
　　Match the vocabulary words to their dictionary definitions.

___ 1. perpetual	A. like early mankind
___ 2. ominously	B. ancient times
___ 3. gander	C. threateningly
___ 4. deed	D. document of ownership
___ 5. perpetrated	E. sexual affairs
___ 6. swindle	F. lacking judgment
___ 7. primitive	G. never ending
___ 8. antiquity	H. committed
___ 9. improvident	I. look
___ 10. fornications	J. scam

VOCABULARY - *A Streetcar Named Desire*

Scene 3 Part I: Using Prior Knowledge and Contextual Clues

Below are the sentences in which the vocabulary words appear in the text. Read the sentence. Use any clues you can find in the sentence combined with your prior knowledge, and write what you think the underlined words mean on the lines provided.

1. The kitchen now suggests that sort of lurid nocturnal brilliance . . .

_____

2. The kitchen now suggests that sort of lurid nocturnal brilliance . . .

_____

3. . . . they are men at the peak of their physical manhood, as coarse and direct and powerful as the primary colors.

_____

4. There are vivid slices of watermelon on the table . . .

_____

5. The bedroom is relatively dim with only the light that spills between the portieres and through the wide window on the street.

_____

6. She raises her arms and stretches, as she moves indolently back to the chair.

_____

7. Rhumba music comes over the radio.

_____

8. . . . reading with feigned difficulty . . .

_____

9. We are French by extraction.

_____

A Streetcar Named Desire Vocabulary Worksheet Scene 3 Continued

10. He coughs diffidently.

_____

Part II: Determining the Meaning
 Match the vocabulary words to their dictionary definitions.

___ 1. lurid   A. lazily
___ 2. nocturnal   B. pretended
___ 3. coarse   C. timidly
___ 4. vivid   D. horrible
___ 5. portieres   E. Cuban dance
___ 6. indolently   F. lineage; from what people one has come
___ 7. rhumba   G. intense
___ 8. feigned   H. during darkness
___ 9. extraction   I. heavy curtain
___ 10. diffidently   J. natural; unprocessed

VOCABULARY - *A Streetcar Named Desire*

Scene 4 Part I: Using Prior Knowledge and Contextual Clues
   Below are the sentences in which the vocabulary words appear in the text. Read the sentence. Use any clues you can find in the sentence combined with your prior knowledge, and write what you think the underlined words mean on the lines provided.

1. Her eyes and lips have that almost narcotized tranquility that is the faces of Eastern idols.

___

2. Stanley's gaudy pyjamas lie across the threshold of the bathroom.

___

3. I don't understand your indifference.

___

4. Is this a Chinese philosophy you've–cultivated?

___

5. I take it for granted that you still have sufficient memories of Belle Reve.

___

6. I can't believe you're in earnest.

___

7. May I–speak–plainly?

___

8. Well–if you forgive me–he's common!

___

9. There's something downright–bestial–about him!

___

A Streetcar Named Desire Vocabulary Worksheet Scene 4 Continued

10. . . . who has listened <u>gravely</u> to Blanche.

_____

Part II: Determining the Meaning
    Match the vocabulary words to their dictionary definitions.

___	1. tranquility	A. showy
___	2. gaudy	B. uncensored
___	3. indifference	C. lack of concern
___	4. cultivated	D. peace
___	5. sufficient	E. inhuman
___	6. earnest	F. ordinary
___	7. plainly	G. tended
___	8. common	H. genuine
___	9. bestial	I. enough
___	10. gravely	J. seriously

VOCABULARY - *A Streetcar Named Desire*

Scene 5 Part I: Using Prior Knowledge and Contextual Clues

Below are the sentences in which the vocabulary words appear in the text. Read the sentence. Use any clues you can find in the sentence combined with your prior knowledge, and write what you think the underlined words mean on the lines provided.

1. And who knows, perhaps I shall take a sudden notion to swoop down on Dallas!

___

2. She and Steve had a row.

___

3. [contemptuously] Hah!

___

4. You hate me to talk sentimental.

___

5. –he thinks I'm sort of–prim and proper, you know.

___

6. This doesn't always work./ It's temperamental?

___

7. She takes a large gossamer scarf from the trunk. . .

___

8. The young man laughs uncomfortably and stands like a bashful kid.

___

9. The young man clears his throat and looks yearningly at the door.

___

A Streetcar Named Desire Vocabulary Worksheet Scene 5 Continued

10. He <u>beams</u> at her selfconsciously.

_____

Part II: Determining the Meaning
   Match the vocabulary words to their dictionary definitions.

   ___   1. notion   A. idea
   ___   2. row   B. a delicate fabric
   ___   3. contemptuously   C. shy
   ___   4. sentimental   D. emotional
   ___   5. prim   E. with desire
   ___   6. temperamental   F. with hatred
   ___   7. gossamer   G. not consistent; unpredictable
   ___   8. bashful   H. fight
   ___   9. yearningly   I. stiffly proper or precise in manner or appearance
   ___ 10. beams   J. radiates

VOCABULARY - *A Streetcar Named Desire*

Scene 6 Part I: Using Prior Knowledge and Contextual Clues

Below are the sentences in which the vocabulary words appear in the text. Read the sentence. Use any clues you can find in the sentence combined with your prior knowledge, and write what you think the underlined words mean on the lines provided.

1. The utter exhaustion which only a neurasthenic personality can know is evident in Blanche's voice and manner.

   _____

2. I've made such a dismal mess of it.

   _____

3. It was the other–familiarity–that I felt obliged to–discourage.

   _____

4. You have been so anxious and solemn all evening. . . .

   _____

5. –I want to create– joie de vivre!

   _____

6. Blanche speaks with an affectation of demureness.

   _____

7. Blanche speaks with an affectation of demureness.

   _____

8. Her voice sounds gently reproving.

   _____

9. He is insufferably rude.

   _____

A Streetcar Named Desire Vocabulary Worksheet Scene 6 Continued

10. There was something different about the boy, a nervousness, a softness and a tenderness which wasn't like a man's, although he wasn't the least bit <u>effeminate</u> looking.

_____

Part II: Determining the Meaning
   Match the vocabulary words to their dictionary definitions.

   ___ 1. neurasthenic   A. fakeness
   ___ 2. dismal   B. know well
   ___ 3. familiarity   C. anxious
   ___ 4. solemn   D. disastrous
   ___ 5. joie de vivre   E. serious
   ___ 6. affectation   F. modesty
   ___ 7. demureness   G. full of life
   ___ 8. reproving   H. feminine
   ___ 9. insufferably   I. criticizing
   ___ 10. effeminate   J. unbearably

VOCABULARY - *A Streetcar Named Desire*

Scene 7 Part I: Using Prior Knowledge and Contextual Clues
   Below are the sentences in which the vocabulary words appear in the text. Read the sentence. Use any clues you can find in the sentence combined with your prior knowledge, and write what you think the underlined words mean on the lines provided.

1. I reckon so.

_____

2. I've got the dope on your big sister, Stella.

_____

3. Blanche is singing in the bathroom a saccharine popular ballad . . .

_____

4. What–contemptible–lies!

_____

5. Blanche's voice is lifted again, serenely as a bell.

_____

6. The distant piano goes into a hectic breakdown.

_____

Part II: Determining the Meaning
   Match the vocabulary words to their dictionary definitions.

___ 1. reckon   A. calmly
___ 2. dope   B. gossip
___ 3. saccharine   C. overly sweet
___ 4. contemptible   D. chaotic
___ 5. serenely   E. figure
___ 6. hectic   F. worthy of hate

VOCABULARY - *A Streetcar Named Desire*

Scene 8 Part I: Using Prior Knowledge and Contextual Clues

Below are the sentences in which the vocabulary words appear in the text. Read the sentence. Use any clues you can find in the sentence combined with your prior knowledge, and write what you think the underlined words mean on the lines provided.

1. I like them when they're amusing but not indecent.

___

2. I must run through my repertoire!

___

3. This old maid . . . knew more vulgar expressions than Mr. Kowalski!

___

4. Stella also makes an ineffectual effort to seem amused.

___

5. Their upstairs neighbors are heard in bellowing laughter at something.

___

6. She pauses reflectively for a moment.

___

7. Then he speaks slowly and with false amiability.

___

8. Hoity-toity, describing me as an ape.

___

9. He is with her now, supporting her with his arm, murmuring indistinguishably as they go outside.

___

58

A Streetcar Named Desire Vocabulary Worksheet Scene 8 Continued

Part II: Determining the Meaning
    Match the vocabulary words to their dictionary definitions.

   ___ 1. indecent   A. friendliness
   ___ 2. repertoire   B. seemingly superior
   ___ 3. expressions   C. roaring
   ___ 4. ineffectual   D. improper
   ___ 5. bellowing   E. collection
   ___ 6. reflectively   F. unsatisfactory; not effective
   ___ 7. amiability   G. thoughtfully
   ___ 8. hoity-toity   H. not understandable; not clear
   ___ 9. indistinguishably   I. sayings

VOCABULARY - *A Streetcar Named Desire*

Scene 9 Part I: Using Prior Knowledge and Contextual Clues

Below are the sentences in which the vocabulary words appear in the text. Read the sentence. Use any clues you can find in the sentence combined with your prior knowledge, and write what you think the underlined words mean on the lines provided.

1. Blanche is seated in a tense hunched position in a bedroom chair.

___

2. Mitch [hoarsely]: Me. Mitch.

___

3. I really shouldn't let you in after the treatment I have received from you this evening! So utterly uncavalier!

___

4. My, my what a cold shoulder! And such uncouth apparel!

___

5. He says you been lapping it up all summer like a wild-cat!

___

6. That pitch about your ideals being so old-fashioned and all the malarkey that you've dished out all summer.

___

7. That pitch about your ideals being so old-fashioned and all the malarkey that you've dished out all summer.

___

8. But I was a fool enough to believe you was straight.

___

A Streetcar Named Desire Vocabulary Worksheet Scene 9 Continued

9. I thanked God for you, because you seemed to be gentle–a <u>cleft</u> in the rock of the world that I could hide in!

_____

10. . . . Mitch turns and goes out the outer door, <u>clatters</u> awkwardly down the steps. . . .

_____

Part II: Determining the Meaning
    Match the vocabulary words to their dictionary definitions.

___	1. hunched	A. bent over; crouched
___	2. hoarsely	B. discourteous
___	3. uncavalier	C. drinking up, like a dog
___	4. uncouth	D. foolish talk
___	5. lapping	E. hollowed area
___	6. pitch	F. set talk designed to persuade
___	7. malarkey	G. crude; rough; unpolished
___	8. straight	H. with a strained voice
___	9. cleft	I. truthful
___	10. clatters	J. to move rapidly and noisily

VOCABULARY - *A Streetcar Named Desire*

Scene 10 Part I: Using Prior Knowledge and Contextual Clues
    Below are the sentences in which the vocabulary words appear in the text. Read the sentence. Use any clues you can find in the sentence combined with your prior knowledge, and write what you think the underlined words mean on the lines provided.

1. . . . a mood of hysterical exhilaration came into her . . . .

   _____

2. . . . she is . . . murmuring excitedly as if to a group of spectral admirers.

   _____

3. A cultivated woman, a woman of intelligence and breeding, can enrich a man's life–immeasurably!

   _____

4. Physical beauty is passing . . . A transitory possession.

   _____

5. How strange that I should be called a destitute woman! When I have all these treasures locked in my heart.

   _____

6. The shadows are of a grotesque and menacing form.

   _____

7. The shadows are of a grotesque and menacing form.

   _____

8. The shadows and lurid reflections move sinuously as flames along the wall spaces.

   _____

A Streetcar Named Desire Vocabulary Worksheet Scene 10 Continued

9. Oh! So you want some rough-house!

_____

10. He picks up her inert figure and carries her to the bed.

_____

Part II: Determining the Meaning
    Match the vocabulary words to their dictionary definitions.

    ___ 1. exhilaration   A. unable to move or act
    ___ 2. spectral   B. unnatural or ugly
    ___ 3. immeasurably   C. curving or twisting
    ___ 4. transitory   D. vast
    ___ 5. destitute   E. feeling of stimulation
    ___ 6. grotesque   F. poor; without necessities
    ___ 7. menacing   G. physical fighting
    ___ 8. sinuously   H. temporary
    ___ 9. rough-house   I. threatening
    ___ 10. inert   J. ghostly

VOCABULARY - *A Streetcar Named Desire*

Scene 11 Part I: Using Prior Knowledge and Contextual Clues

    Below are the sentences in which the vocabulary words appear in the text. Read the sentence. Use any clues you can find in the sentence combined with your prior knowledge, and write what you think the underlined words mean on the lines provided.

1. Stanley [prodigiously elated]: You know what luck is?

___

2. Stanley [prodigiously elated]: You know what luck is?

___

3. I always did say that men are callous things with no feelings, but this does beat anything.

___

4. . . . a look of sorrowful perplexity as though all human experience shows on her face.

___

5. Divested of all the softer properties of womanhood, the matron is a peculiarly sinister figure in her severe dress.

___

6. Divested of all the softer properties of womanhood, the matron is a peculiarly sinister figure in her severe dress.

___

7. The greeting is echoed . . . as if reverberated through a canyon of rock.

___

8. Blanche [retreating in panic]: I don't know you–I don't know you.

___

9. The heavy woman pinions her arms.

___

64

A Streetcar Named Desire Vocabulary Worksheet Scene 11 Continued

10. Stanley [voluptuously, soothingly]: Now, honey. Now, love. Now, now, love.

_____

Part II: Determining the Meaning
    Match the vocabulary words to their dictionary definitions.

___ 1. prodigiously	A. wonderfully
___ 2. elated	B. confusion or uncertainty
___ 3. callous	C. going backwards
___ 4. perplexity	D. got rid of
___ 5. sinister	E. sensuously
___ 6. reverberated	F. insensitive
___ 7. divested	G. wrestle; hold down
___ 8. retreating	H. happy
___ 9. pinions	I. evil
___ 10. voluptuously	J. echoed

VOCABULARY ANSWER KEY *A Streetcar Named Desire*

Scene 1	Scene 2	Scene 3
1. I	1. G	1. D
2. F	2. C	2. H
3. H	3. I	3. J
4. J	4. D	4. G
5. G	5. H	5. I
6. C	6. J	6. A
7. E	7. A	7. E
8. B	8. B	8. B
9. D	9. F	9. F
10. A	10. E	10. C

Scene 4	Scene 5	Scene 6
1. D	1. A	1. C
2. A	2. H	2. D
3. C	3. F	3. B
4. G	4. D	4. E
5. I	5. I	5. G
6. H	6. G	6. A
7. B	7. B	7. F
8. F	8. C	8. I
9. E	9. E	9. J
10. J	10. J	10. H

Scene 7	Scene 8	Scene 9
1. E	1. D	1. A
2. B	2. E	2. H
3. C	3. I	3. B
4. F	4. F	4. G
5. A	5. C	5. C
6. D	6. G	6. F
	7. A	7. D
	8. B	8. I
	9. H	9. E
		10. J

Scene 10	Scene 11	
1. E	1. A	
2. J	2. H	
3. D	3. F	
4. H	4. B	
5. F	5. I	
6. B	6. J	
7. I	7. D	
8. C	8. C	
9. G	9. G	
10. A	10. E	

DAILY LESSONS

LESSON ONE

Objectives
1. To introduce the *A Streetcar Named Desire* unit
2. To distribute books and other related materials
3. To preview the study questions for Scene 1
4. To familiarize students with the vocabulary for Scene 1
5. To read Scene 1

Activity #1
Before reading or introducing the play, begin with the following freewrite. You can write it on the board or you can give a handout with the following copied on it. You can collect student responses or just discuss them, or if you use student journals, this can be the first entry. You can allow students to choose which relationship they would like to address, or you can assign them.

Freewrite Prompt:

Relationships are often influenced by our expectations of others. Consider the following roles in relationships:
> husband
> wife
> siblings
> in-laws

Select one of these roles and write 1-2 paragraphs about the "expectations" for that role. In other words, what kinds of responsibilities does that person have, what kinds of attitudes should he or she have, etc.

When students have completed their responses (it should take 4-7 minutes for them to write), ask for volunteers to share their responses. As student share, ask if others agree or disagree with their ideas. This is a good time to remind students about making I-statements (rather than you-statements). Promoting some healthy disagreement will make reading the play more interesting.

Transition: Ask students to keep this question of roles and expectations in mind as you begin reading the play. Ask them to look for latent or manifest statements, relationships, and role expectations occurring in the play.

Activity #2
Distribute the materials students will use in this unit. Explain in detail how students are to use these materials.

Study Guides Students should read the study guide questions for each reading assignment prior to beginning the reading assignment to get a feeling for what events and ideas are important in the section they are about to read. After reading the section, students will (as a class or individually) answer the questions to review the important events and ideas from that section of the book. Students should keep the study guides as study materials for the unit test. **Preview the study questions for Scene 1 while students have their study guides out.**

Vocabulary   Prior to each a reading assignment, students will do vocabulary work related to the section of the book they are about to read. Following the completion of the reading of the book, there will be a vocabulary review of all the words used in the vocabulary assignments. Students should keep their vocabulary work as study materials for the unit test. **Do the worksheet for Scene 1 orally with the class to show students how the worksheets should be done.**

Reading Assignment Sheet   You need to fill in the reading assignment sheet to let students know by when their reading has to be completed. You can either write the assignment sheet up on a side blackboard or bulletin board and leave it there for students to see each day, or you can make copies for each student to have. In either case, you should advise students to become very familiar with the reading assignments so they know what is expected of them.

Extra Activities Center   The Unit Resource Materials portion of this LitPlan contains suggestions for an extra library of related books and articles in your classroom as well as crossword and word search puzzles. Make an extra activities center in your room where you will keep these materials for students to use. (Bring the books and articles in from the library and keep several copies of the puzzles on hand.) Explain to students that these materials are available for students to use when they finish reading assignments or other class work early.

Non-fiction Assignment Sheet   Explain to students that they each are to read at least one non-fiction piece from the in-class library at some time during the unit. Students will fill out a Non-fiction Assignment Sheet after completing the reading to help you (the teacher) evaluate their reading experiences and to help the students think about and evaluate their own reading experiences.

Books   Each school has its own rules and regulations regarding student use of school books. Advise students of the procedures that are normal for your school.

Activity #3
If time permits, the class should begin reading Scene 1 aloud. Suggest that students annotate characters' attitudes towards relationships, roles and expectations, especially those split along gender lines and when characters are purposefully being polite to fulfill the expectations of these roles. If you have not yet completed an oral reading evaluation of your students, this is a good opportunity to do so. An Oral Reading Evaluation form is included for your convenience. Continue doing oral reading and filling out the evaluations until each student has had a chance to read. Then, you may have students read silently, in pairs or groups (to each other), or in whatever way you choose.

Students should complete reading Scene 1 of *A Streetcar Named Desire* prior to your next class.

ORAL READING EVALUATION - *A Streetcar Named Desire*

Name _____ Class____ Date _____

SKILL	EXCELLENT	GOOD	AVERAGE	FAIR	POOR
Fluency	5	4	3	2	1
Clarity	5	4	3	2	1
Audibility	5	4	3	2	1
Pronunciation	5	4	3	2	1
_____	5	4	3	2	1
_____	5	4	3	2	1

Total ____ Grade ____

Comments:

LESSON TWO

Objectives
    1. To review the main ideas and events of Scene 1
    2. To understand characterization by examining text carefully
    3. To do the prereading and reading work for Scene 2

Activity #1
Give students a few minutes to formulate answers for the study guide questions for Scene 1, and then discuss the answers to the questions in detail. Write the answers on the board or overhead transparency so students can have the correct answers for study purposes. After you discuss the questions for Scene 1, preview the questions for Scene 2.

NOTE: It is a good practice in public speaking and leadership skills for individual students to take charge of leading the discussions of the study questions. Perhaps a different student could go to the front of the class and lead the discussion each day that the study questions are discussed in this unit. Of course, you should guide the discussion when appropriate and try to fill in any gaps students may leave. The study questions could really be handled in a number of different ways, including in small groups with group reports following. Occasionally you may want to use the multiple choice questions as quizzes to check students' reading comprehension. As a short review now and then, students could pair up for the first (or last, if you have time left at the end of a class period) few minutes of class to quiz each other from the study questions. Mix up methods of reviewing the materials and checking comprehension throughout the unit so students don't get bored just answering the questions the same way each day. Variety in methods will also help address the different learning styles of your students. From now on in this unit, the directions will simply say, "Discuss the answers to the study questions in detail as previously directed." You will choose the method of preparation and discussion each day based on what best suits you and your class.

Activity #2
Distribute the Character Examination Chart. Ask students to find 3-4 details for each box for the characters of Stanley, Stella, and Blanche. Students can work independently, in pairs, or small groups. You can also assign groups to focus on a single character. After students have ample time to complete the assignment, you should meet back as a whole class and discuss the students' answers. Note that students should independently fill out the boxes for Mitch and Eunice as they read further, and tell students to continue to look for additional character information about Stanley, Stella, and Blanche as they read more of the play.

Activity #3
Give students time to complete the vocabulary worksheet for Scene 2. Post the answers to the worksheet on the board for the next class meeting so students can come in and check their own papers at the beginning of class. Do this each day that students have vocabulary work (if your students are at a level where they can do this independently). It will save class time for other activities.

Activity #4
Begin reading Scene 2 aloud. Continue the oral reading evaluations. Students should complete this assignment prior to the next class meeting.

CHARACTER EXAMINATION CHART - *A Streetcar Named Desire*

Character	Physical Description	Characteristics (mannerisms, personality flaws, etc.)	Key Phrases from the text (ex. "animal joy" for Stanley and "radiant smile" for Stella)
Stanley			
Stella			
Blanche			
Mitch			
Eunice			

LESSON THREE

Objectives
1. To review the main ideas and events of Scene 2
2. To preview the study questions and do the vocabulary work for Scene 3
3. To read Scene 3
4. To give students an opportunity to express their opinions about literature based on textual evidence
5. To evaluate students' writing

Activity #1
Give students a few minutes to review Scene 2 or ask questions if they have any. Give them a Scene 2 quiz.

Activity #2
Discuss the answers to the quizzes and study questions for Scene 2 as previously directed.

Activity #3
Ask students to skim Scene 2 quickly and write down uses of the words "man" or "boy." Blanche uses these words rather deliberately. Ask students if they see a difference in the way she uses these words. According to Blanche, which is Stanley, a "man" or a "boy"?

Activity #4
Tell students that prior to the next class period that they should have completed the prereading and reading work for Scene 3. Ask them to continue paying attention to the tension between "man" and "boy" and "man" and "woman" that they see emerging in the text.

Activity #5
Distribute Writing Assignment #1. Discuss the directions in detail and tell students when the assignment must be turned in.

Activity #6
Give students the remainder of this class time to begin the prereading and reading work for Scene 3.

WRITING ASSIGNMENT #1 - *A Streetcar Named Desire*

PROMPT
In Scenes 3 and 4, Tennessee Williams explores domestic abuse in the play when Stanley strikes Stella offstage. Stella's initial response is to leave, though she later has a change of heart and returns, a decision which mystifies Blanche. Imagine Stella and Blanche have another sister. You will adopt the persona of this sister and write Stella a letter which advises her on what to do about her marital situation. You can assume that you know all the details of the play, as Blanche was afraid and telephoned you to ask for your advice.

In short, your letter should either suggest that Stella stay in the relationship or leave it. Then, your letter should give advice: should she move away, try to pacify Stanley, learn how to defend herself, or what? As you give advice and share your personal opinions, be sure to show your knowledge of the play by adding important details. Also, make sure that you address the role of love in the Kowalskis' relationship. Do you think Stanley truly loves Stella? Does Stella truly love Stanley? Use details from the play to support your claims. Your letter should be 4-6 paragraphs.

PREWRITING
The first task is to make sure you understand Stella's attitude toward Stanley. You should skim the scenes and make note of moments when she voices satisfaction or dissatisfaction with her marriage.

DRAFTING
Your first paragraph should explain your perception of the Stella's conflict and why she has kept the details of her life with Stanley largely a secret from her family. This paragraph should also explain your personal opinion of the situation and clearly indicate if you advise Stella to try to work things out or to leave the marriage.

Your body paragraphs should explain different criteria for your advice; for example, are love and loyalty important, or safety, or Stella's unborn child? You should also use details from the play to support your reasoning. For example, has Stella demonstrated love for Stanley, or merely obligation?

In your conclusion paragraph you should summarize your hopes for Stella and emphasize your view of her and how she has changed during the marriage. Be sure you use the proper formatting for your letter.

PROOFREADING
When you finish the rough draft of your letter, ask a student who sits near you to read it. After reading your rough draft, he/she should tell you what he/she liked best about your work, which parts were difficult to understand, and ways in which your work could be improved. Reread your letter considering your critic's comments, and make the corrections you think are necessary.

Do a final proofreading of your letter double-checking your grammar, spelling, organization, and the clarity of your ideas.

WRITING EVALUATION FORM - *A Streetcar Named Desire*

Name _____ Date _____

Grade _____

Circle One For Each Item:

Grammar: correct   errors noted on paper

Spelling: correct   errors noted on paper

Punctuation: correct   errors noted on paper

Legibility: excellent   good   fair   poor

_____   excellent   good   fair   poor

_____   excellent   good   fair   poor

Strengths:

Weaknesses:

Comments/Suggestions:

LESSON FOUR

Objectives
    1. To assess students' independent reading of Scene 3
    2. To practice taking assessments
    3. To practice understanding metaphor
    4. To preview the study questions, do the vocabulary work for, and read Scene 4

Activity #1
Quiz - Distribute quizzes for Scene 3 and give students about 10 minutes to complete them. Collect papers for grading.

Activity #2
Discuss the answers to the study questions for Scene 3 as previously directed. Preview the study questions for Scene 4 while students have their study questions out.

Activity #3
Invite students to write questions they may have pertaining to any aspect of the play on the board. Everyone must add one question. Use this as a point of departure for discussion.

Activity #4
Break into small groups. Distribute paper and markers to each group. They should brainstorm a list of terms and ideas about the game poker. These questions may help prompt students:
    What are the rules?
    What is the objective of the game?
    What skills are required?
    What makes a player "good" or not?
    What is bluffing?
When students have exhausted their ideas, have each group report to the class. As a whole group, identify the 3 most important discoveries students made and try to connect them to Scene 3.

Activity #4
Ask students to answer the following question in their reading journal/log or notes:
    How does poker relate to the play's theme of lying?

Activity #5
Tell students that prior to the next class period they should complete the vocabulary and reading work for Scene 4. Remind them to be thinking about and working on Writing Assignment #1.

LESSON FIVE

Objectives
1. To review the main ideas and events from Scene 4
2. To practice connecting literature to real-life experiences
3. To trace the development of a theme
4. To do the prereading and reading work for chapters Scene 5

Activity #1
Discuss the answers to the study questions for Scene 4 as previously directed. Have students preview the questions for Scene 5 while they have their study guides out.

Activity #2
Today in class, students will explore the theme of making assumptions about others, as Blanche presumptuously makes assumptions about Stella's lifestyle.

Have students write a 1-2 paragraph response to the following prompt:

Think of a time when you made assumptions about someone else's business or felt that you knew better about their circumstances than the other person–or when someone felt this way toward you. What were the consequences of making these assumptions?

After 5-7 minutes, ask volunteers to share their writing, either by reading or summarizing.

After sharing, give students 10 minutes to write about how Blanche may be making assumptions about Stella and Stanley. Ask students to locate a place in the text where they see Blanche doing this, and have them write about the language of that passage.

You can use these questions as prompts: Are Blanche's assumptions valid? Does Blanche see the whole picture when it comes to Stanley and Stella, or only part of it? Why? Are there consequences to this?

Activity #3
Tell students that prior to the next class period they should have completed the vocabulary and reading work for Scene 5. Students may use the remainder of this period to begin this assignment.

Remind students to be working on Writing Assignment #1. Any extra time can be spent conferencing with students or allowing students to discuss their progress on the assignment.

LESSON SIX

Objectives
1. To review the main ideas and events from Scene 5
2. To use close passage analysis as the basis for group discussion
3. To learn about meaning created through juxtaposition
4. To do the prereading work for Scene 6

Activity #1
Discuss the answers to the study questions for Scene 5 as previously directed. Have students preview the questions for Scene 6 while they have their study guides out.

Activity #2
Today the class will investigate the concept of juxtaposition. Introduce the word and define it. Most simply, juxtaposition is the meaning created when two concepts are placed side by side. This scene juxtaposes Mitch and the newspaper boy. By creating this juxtaposition, Williams is suggesting some meaning, and the class will get at this in small groups.

Get into small groups of 3-4 students. First, very carefully look at the final pages of the scene, focusing on the interaction between Blanche and the paperboy. Work together to annotate the passage, selecting words that seem especially important and might have double meanings. Take note, too, of the very end of the scene: Mitch enters, and we see Blanche's reaction. This is the moment of juxtaposition. At this moment, consider and discuss the following questions:

- How does Blanche perceive the paperboy and Mitch?
- Does she relate to them in different ways?
- How does Blanche behave toward the paperboy? Toward Mitch?
- What does this show us about Blanche?

Activity #3
Tell students that prior to the next class period they should complete the vocabulary work for Scene 6. Students may use the remainder of this class period to begin on this assignment.

LESSON SEVEN

Objectives
    1. To read Scene 6
    2. To review the main ideas and events from Scene 6
    3. To do the prereading and reading work for Scene 7
    4. To practice reading out loud
    5. To give teachers an opportunity to evaluate oral reading skills

Activity #1
Have students read Scene 6 of *A Streetcar Named Desire* out loud in class. Continue the oral reading evaluations if you have not yet completed them.

Activity #2
While reading aloud, appoint some students who don't have reading parts to have "thinking parts." For example, one student reads Blanche's lines aloud and another is responsible for figuring out what Blanche is actually feeling and thinking. At random intervals (using an egg timer works well), call on the "thinker" for the corresponding "reader" of the passage just read aloud to explain what the "reader" is actually "thinking." This exercise helps students practice reading between the lines in a more habitual way. Also, some students could be assigned to raise their hands when they think the next study question has been answered in the text. All students can make notes and complete their worksheets as you read.

Activity #3
Discuss the answers to the study questions for Scene 6 as previously directed. Have students preview the questions for Scene 7 while they have their study guides out.

Activity #4
Tell students that prior to the next class period they should have completed the vocabulary and reading work for Scene 7. Students may use the remainder of this period to begin this assignment.

LESSON EIGHT

Objectives
1. To review the main ideas and events from Scene 7
2. To assess independent reading skills
3. To better understand characterization
4. To do the prereading and reading work for Scene 8

Activity #1
Give students a quiz on Scene 7. Use the multiple choice form of the study guide questions as a quiz so that in discussing the answers to the quiz you also answer the study guide questions. Collect the quizzes to record the grades.

Activity #2
Materials Needed
Give each student a piece of construction paper and art materials, including colored pencils, markers, magazines for clipping, scissors, glue and so on.

Students will fold their papers in half, like a greeting card. Students will make a birthday card for Blanche. It can be silly or serious, as long as it shows relevance to Blanche's character. Each student must write a verse for inside the card, with a minimum of 8 lines. For example, the card's verse might compare Blanche's beauty to a moonlit night. Students should write "Designed By [student name]" on the back of the card.

When students are through creating their cards (possibly after 15-20 minutes), take the cards and place them on the ledge of the blackboard. Then, students will "shop" for a card made by a class mate. Then, students should imagine that they are either Stella, Stanley or Mitch, and write a birthday message in the card for Blanche. Again, the message should be relevant to Blanche's character, as well as reveal something about the character "giving" the card. Students should write "Given By [student name]" on the back of the card.

Students should exchange cards. Have students fold a sheet of notebook paper in quarters. They should now assume the persona of Blanche. Having received the birthday card, she should write a thank you note back to the person, telling her reaction to the card. Students should write "Note Written By [student name]" on the back of the thank you note. Students should give their thank you notes back to the people who gave them the birthday cards.

The birthday cards should have the appropriate notes that go with them inserted. Collect the cards and notes for grading and display.

Activity #3
Tell students that prior to the next class meeting they must complete the vocabulary and reading work for Scene 8. If time remains in this class period, they may begin working on the assignments.

LESSON NINE

Objectives
1. To review the main ideas and events from Scene 8
2. To practice taking assessments
3. To give students an opportunity to convey facts in their writing
4. To give teachers an opportunity to evaluate student writing
5. To do the prereading and reading work for Scene 9

Activity #1
Give students a few minutes to review Scene 8 or ask questions if they have any. Give them a Scene 8 quiz. Prior to the quiz, you might invite students to put their questions about the novel on the board, as a prompt for review.

Activity #2
Discuss the answers to the study questions for Scene 8 as previously directed. Preview the study questions for Scene 9 while students have their study guides out.

Activity #3
Distribute Writing Assignment #2 and the Non-fiction Reading Assignment. Discuss the directions in detail and assign a due date when the article must be read by and when the essay is due.

The Non-fiction Reading Assignment will be linked to this writing assignment, which will be based on the content of the article. The next class period will be dedicated to locating a relevant article and reading it closely.

Note: Schedule time in the library or computer lab for article research.

Activity #4
Use the remainder of the class period for students to work independently completing the vocabulary and reading work for Scene 9. Students should complete reading Scene 9 for homework, even though they may be conducting article research during the next class.

Additionally, students should have a topic for Writing Assignment #2 in mind when they arrive to the next class.

WRITING ASSIGNMENT #2 - *A Streetcar Named Desire*

PROMPT
You will be writing an essay that informs your reader about a social issue. Your essay is not meant to persuade, but to educate your reader using facts. *A Streetcar Named Desire* incorporates many serious themes, such as several forms of discrimination. You will write an essay that profiles an actual incident when someone suffered discrimination on the basis of age, race, sex, class or sexual orientation. You should properly quote the information you use from your article. Your essay should be 4-5 paragraphs in length and should address the essential questions: who, what, where, when, why and how.

PREWRITING
Begin by thinking about what topic–age, race, sex, class, or sexual orientation–you might be interested in exploring. Is there one which seems more important or relevant to you or your community?

Once you select a topic area, for example, discrimination based on sex, begin to think about related issues. One major example of discrimination toward women in America is that women were denied the right to vote until the 1920s. This is an issue that you can explore, using database search engines or the internet. You might search using keywords like suffrage. As you turn up results, consider the multiple options which you could make the focus of your essay. You might write about a well-known activist or about how the constitutional amendment for women's right to vote was passed. You should collect a few articles, but focus on one to use when completing your Non-fiction Reading Assignment.

Once you have read your primary article closely, read it again and make notes on the most relevant points in the article. Your notes can be direct quotes or paraphrases, but be sure to keep track of which words are yours and which are the author's.

DRAFTING
Write an introductory paragraph in which you introduce the subject of your article and state the purpose of your essay, which is to inform your audience about this particular form of discrimination. In the body of your essay, you should address the most relevant who/what/why/where/when/ how questions to your topic. You might define the form of discrimination in a paragraph early in the essay. Also, be sure to convey who is practicing this discrimination and, perhaps, why. Be sure to explain what the consequences of this discrimination are–is someone being harmed, is it affecting the community, is it resulting in crime or loss of liberty? Be sure to quote any information you gleaned from your articles accurately.

In your concluding paragraph, revisit each of your main points and summarize them.

A Streetcar Named Desire Writing Assignment #2 Page 2

Then, explain why the incident you profiled is an act of discrimination. Remember that your essay is to inform, not persuade; your personal opinion should not be included, however reprehensible the discrimination may be.

PROMPT
When you finish the rough draft of your paper, ask a student who sits near you to read it. After reading your rough draft, he/she should tell you what he/she liked best about your work, which parts were difficult to understand, and ways in which your work could be improved. Reread your paper considering your critic's comments, and make the corrections you think are necessary.

PROOFREADING
Do a final proofreading of your paper, double-checking your grammar, spelling, organization, and the clarity of your ideas.

NON-FICTION ASSIGNMENT SHEET
(To be completed after reading the required nonfiction article)

Name _____ Date _____

Title of Nonfiction Read _____

Written By _____ Publication Date _____

I. Factual Summary: Write a short summary of the piece you read.

II. Vocabulary
    1. With which vocabulary words in the piece did you encounter some degree of difficulty?

    2. How did you resolve your lack of understanding with these words?

III. Interpretation: What was the main point the author wanted you to get from reading his work?

IV. Criticism
    1. With which points of the piece did you agree or find easy to accept? Why?

    2. With which points of the piece did you disagree or find difficult to believe? Why?

V. Personal Response: What do you think about this piece? OR How does this piece influence your ideas?

WRITING EVALUATION FORM - *A Streetcar Named Desire*

Name _____ Date _____

Grade _____

Circle One For Each Item:

Grammar: correct   errors noted on paper

Spelling: correct   errors noted on paper

Punctuation: correct   errors noted on paper

Legibility: excellent   good   fair   poor

_____   excellent   good   fair   poor

_____   excellent   good   fair   poor

Strengths:

Weaknesses:

Comments/Suggestions:

LESSON TEN

Objectives
1. To practice library research
2. To practice reading comprehension of non-fiction writing
3. To conference about writing with students

Activity #1
Allow students to have the period to do library or internet research to find articles to use in completing Writing Assignment #2 and the non-fiction reading assignment. You might invite the librarian to give a brief overview of how to use library resources effectively.

Activity #2
While students are researching, call individual students to your desk or some other private area for a writing conference based on the first two writing assignments in this unit. The writing evaluation form included in this unit is a good basis for the conference.

Activity #3
Remind students when you plan to collect their assignments.

Activity #4
Students should use the remainder of the class period to complete the Non-fiction Assignment Sheet.

Activity #5
Remind students to complete the prereading and reading work for Scene 9 prior to the next class meeting. They may work on this assignment if they finish their Non-fiction Assignment Sheets early.

LESSON ELEVEN

Objectives
>1. To review the main ideas and events from Scene 9
>2. To do the prereading and reading work for Scene 10
>3. To raise questions about literature and respond in writing

Activity #1
Discuss the answers to the study questions for Scene 9 as previously directed. Have students preview the study questions for Scene 10 while they have their study guides out.

Activity #2
Have students arrange their desks so they are in a circle. If you have more than 20 students in your class, divide the students in half and make two large groups. Have each student take out a clean piece of paper. At the top of the paper, each student should write a question that digs into some aspect of Scene 9 that interests, angers or confuses–the question should not be one from the prereading activities and it should not be obvious. For example, a question might be: Why does Blanche ask Mitch to marry her? Or, why does Mitch attack Blanche? Or, do Blanche and Mitch make a compatible couple?

Once everyone has a question, students should pass their papers to the student on their left. That student addresses the question by writing a statement, question or quote and then passes the paper to his or her left and so on and so on, until the paper comes back to the original student. This activity is best completed in total silence, with occasional teacher prompts that students give thoughtful responses. Give the students a few minutes to read the responses from their peers, and, if time allows, freewrite about how their initial ideas may have changed now that they see others' perspectives.

Activity #3
If time permits, allow students to share their original questions and talk about the responses they received. Students should also consider if their peers' responses have influenced their views.

Activity #4
Tell students that prior to the next class meeting they must complete the vocabulary and reading work for Scene 10.

LESSON TWELVE

Objectives
1. To review the main ideas and events from Scene 10
2. To do the prereading and reading work for Scene 11
3. To assess independent reading skills
4. To think conceptually about symbols

Activity #1
Give students a quiz on Scene 10. Use either the short answer or multiple choice form of the study guide questions as a quiz so that in discussing the answers to the quiz you also answer the study guide questions. Collect the quizzes to record the grades.

Activity #2
Ask students to skim Scene 10. While skimming, they should make a list of important objects mentioned in the scene, working independently. One example is Blanche's tiara. Students should have 10-15 objects on their lists, and not more (more leads to adding indiscriminately to their lists). Allot about 10 minutes to compile these lists.

Then, ask students to identify the three objects that they perceive as the most important.

Then, they must select one object and write a paragraph about what the symbol represents and why it is the most important symbol in the scene.

Activity #3
Get into small groups of 2-3 students and share results.

Activity #4
Report back to the whole class after 3-4 minutes. Facilitate a discussion that connects the symbols to characters: How does the symbol suggest a change in the character? What does the symbol indicate about a character's motivation?

Activity #5
Tell students that prior to the next class meeting they must complete the vocabulary and reading work for Scene 11.

LESSON THIRTEEN

Objectives
    1. To review the main ideas and events from Scene 11
    2. To practice taking assessments
    3. To practice close passage analysis
    4. To learn about denotation and connotation
    5. To give the teacher an opportunity to assess a project/piece of writing

Activity #1
Give students a quiz on Scene 11 Use either the short answer or multiple choice form of the study guide questions as a quiz so that in discussing the answers to the quiz you also answer the study guide questions. Collect the quizzes to record the grades.

Activity #2
Distribute the worksheet for close passage analysis (on the following page). Read it over together carefully.

Activity #3
As a class, reread the last two pages of the play together out loud. Ask students to annotate as they go, taking note of words and phrases which they think are significant.

Activity #4
Have students select a passage from the final two pages and write a one-paragraph close passage analysis of it, concentrating on connotation and denotation. Students may use the sample paragraph from the worksheet as a model. They should write about how particular words, phrases, figures of speech and images create meaning within the passage. Students should also think of any connections between their passage and passages from earlier in the play.

Activity #5
(Optional) Distribute the Project Assignment Sheet and discuss the expectations of the assignment. Assign a clear due date and/or dedicate in-class time to completing the project.

WORKSHEET FOR CLOSE PASSAGE ANALYSIS *A Streetcar Named Desire*

Close Passage Analysis is an important skill for you to develop as a student. When you analyze a passage closely you are singling out words and phrases that are especially important and identifying any important figures of speech. Then you are explaining and interpreting these words and phrases to show why they are significant. So, Close Passage Analysis begins with annotation, then observation, then analysis and explanation.

When writers write they can choose any word from thousands of words, so the words a writer decides to put down on a page together are significant choices. As readers who want to dig deeply into meaning, we must realize how important individual words can be.

Consider the following example:

Row, row, row your boat,
Gently down the stream.
Merrily, merrily, merrily, merrily,
Life is but a dream.

Consider this example:

Propel, Propel, Propel your craft
Placidly down the liquid solution
Ecstatically, ecstatically, ecstatically, ecstatically,
Existence is but an illusion.

While the meaning of the examples above may be technically the same, the words themselves create different meanings. Words all have a denotation and a connotation. **Denotation** is the literal, dictionary definition of a word. **Connotation** is any meaning beyond the literal meaning. So, how does the connotation differ between the two versions of the song? Is there a difference in meaning? What is it?

How to Write About Your Discoveries

Let's imagine we are writing a paper about "Row, Row, Row." We are arguing that it is actually a song about how work is what makes life fulfilling. Here's how we would prove this, using close passage analysis in our writing:

The song suggests that work and labor are what makes life fulfilling. Note the repetition of the word "row." Rowing is a very physical activity that requires exertion. Without the consistent application of this work (rowing), one cannot become "merry." Notice the repetition of "merrily." The repetition suggests a relationship with the only other repeated word, "row." Perhaps one must "row" to become "merry." Once this status is achieved, "life becomes a dream." Perhaps the author means that through hard work, one can achieve a "dream" or state of satisfaction, contentment and fulfillment.

PROJECT ASSIGNMENT - *A Streetcar Named Desire*

PROMPT
Just like we collect memories of our experiences, we literally collect the "stuff" of our lives. These things—photographs, garments, trophies, souvenirs, letters, gifts and other odds and ends—are the mementos and treasures of our lives, and they tell a story about us.

You will be creating a time capsule that celebrates your youth. You must think of five objects that you would place in a time capsule that represents your childhood. Instead of actually placing your items in a time capsule, you will either photograph or photocopy them.

For each object you select, you must write two paragraphs. One paragraph should explain the object itself. Describe it, explain how you received it, tell where you keep it, share who gave it to you and so on. In the second paragraph, explain why the item has symbolic value to you and why it belongs in your time capsule. Be sure to explain how it symbolizes your youth.

You can present your photographs or photocopies and your corresponding paragraphs on a poster board display, in a report folder, as a PowerPoint file, or web page.

You will present your time capsule to the class, explaining the objects and their meanings. Your presentation will be brief, only 3-5 minutes.

REQUIREMENTS
1. Five visual (photograph or photocopy) representations of your time capsule objects
2. Five corresponding paragraphs describing your items.
3. Five corresponding paragraphs explaining the significance of your items.

PROMPT
Practice your presentation with a partner. Ask your partner to make a list of three points of constructive criticism. Give your partner the same courtesy, so you can both improve your presentations. Make sure that your presentation is about 3-5 minutes long.

LESSON FOURTEEN

<u>Objectives</u>
   1. To review the main characters of the novel
   2. To read closely to understand characterization
   3. To practice improvisational speaking

<u>Activity #1</u>
One way to understand a character is to step into that character's shoes. In this character improvisation exercise, students will answer questions according to how they believe the character would answer, based on their knowledge of the character. Before class, put each student's name on a slip of paper and place in a "fishbowl" to draw at random later.

Begin by dividing the class into four groups: Stella, Stanley, Blanche, and Mitch. You can assign groups or have students count off or self-select.

Give students 15 minutes to go through the text and their study guide questions to get a sense of who their assigned character is. They should jot down a list of 10 facts about their character as well as a list of 10 descriptive adjectives about the character. For example, a fact about Blanche is that she previously lived in a grand home. A descriptive adjective that applies to Blanche is flirtatious. This can be completed independently or in the corresponding groups.

<u>Activity #2</u>
Once students have completed their lists, you will begin the improvisation. Select a name from the "fishbowl" and ask that student to answer one of the following questions "in character." The student can answer from his or her seat or act out his or her reply, depending on how much time you would like to invest in the activity. Also, the assignment can be given first as homework, allowing students time to bring in props to "act out" their assigned character the next day. These changes can be made at the teacher's discretion. It is ok, interesting even, to use a question more than once. The variety of responses yields a rich new way to view characters. The answers to these questions are not necessarily found in the text, so students should formulate answers based on their awareness of a character's traits.

Questions for Improvisations:
- What was your childhood like?
- What was the happiest moment of your life?
- What are your hopes for the future?
- What causes you to feel fear?
- What one possession is the most important to you?
- Do you think it is important to be liked by other people?
- What is your greatest strength?
- What is your greatest weakness?
- What do you wish you could change about yourself?
- Do you have any regrets?
- How can you change the world for the better?
- How do you define success?
- How do you define failure?

LESSON FIFTEEN

<u>Objectives</u>
    1. To discuss *A Streetcar Named Desire* at an in-depth, analytical level
    2. To practice responding to brief essay questions
    3. To practice learning collaboratively
    4. To prepare for an in-class writing activity to be completed during the next class

<u>Activity #1</u>
Break your class into 4 or 5 groups. Assign each group a different question from the Extra Writing Assignments/Discussion Questions. Give the group about five minutes to discuss the question. Then, each student should take about ten minutes and write down his or her own answer to the question.

Shuffle up your groups: form new groups with one representative for each question. Let each student report to the new group about his or her own question. As students teach each other, encourage students to take notes.

Have everyone return to his or her seat. Ask if anyone has questions about the material they just reviewed.

<u>Activity #2</u>
Introduce Writing Assignment #3, which will be completed during the next class period with a time limit. This will allow students to practice timed writing. The in-class writing exercise will require students to select three passages from the play that they see as related in some way. In their essays they will explain the connections they see and explore the significance of the connection.

Emphasize that students must prepare in advance for their in-class essay–they must bring a sheet with three different quotes from the play written on it. Emphasize that their success will depend on the quality of thinking they invest in selecting their passages. Hastily selected passages will not work successfully for this assignment.

<u>Activity #3</u>
If time permits, brainstorm a list of major themes on the board to spur students into thinking about connections between different passages in the play.

EXTRA DISCUSSION QUESTIONS/WRITING ASSIGNMENTS

Interpretation
1. Who are the secondary characters in the play? What function do they serve?
2. Why does aging seem to affect women more than men in this play?
3. How does the setting contribute to meaning in the play?
4. Are the locations of the American South and, more specifically, New Orleans significant?
5. Does Stanley justify his actions? How?
6. One of the topics the play explores is mental illness. How is it shown, and what point is made about it?
7. How does materialism influence characters in the play?
8. Is there a double standard for what behaviors are appropriate for men and women?
9. Is there a relationship between characters' reputations and how others treat them? If so, explain how, giving specific examples from the play.
10. What are three major conflicts in the play? Are they resolved? If so, how?
11. Which characters are guilty of lying or misrepresentation?
12. Choose a main character and tell whether or not that character's past influence his or her present.

Critical
13. Why did Stella "gloss" descriptions of her life in her letters to Blanche?
14. Why is poker a dominant motif? What does it show us about Stanley or men in general?
15. Why is bathing and creating one's personal appearance so central to the play?
16. Why did Blanche kiss the paperboy?
17. What do the shadows represent? Why do they appear again in the final scene?
18. How does physical beauty relate to power in the play?
19. How does virility relate to power in the play?
20. How does sexuality relate to power in the play?
21. Compare and contrast Stanley and Blanche.
22. Compare and contrast Stella and Blanche.
23. How does the play's title relate to the themes of *A Streetcar Named Desire*?

Critical/Personal Response
24. Do you think Stanley is a good husband?
25. Do you think Stella is a good sister?
26. Is Stanley attractive or repulsive, or both?
27. Is Stella content with her life?
28. Do you think Mitch behaves honorably?
29. Is it the rape, or some other factor, that contributes to Blanche's rapid decline?
30. Who or what should be blamed for the loss of Belle Reve?
31. Why is it significant that Stella is pregnant? How is this detail symbolic?
32. Compare and contrast the Kowalski household with the way you think things would have been at Belle Reve.

A Streetcar Named Desire Extra Discussion Questions Page 2

Critical/Personal Response Continued
33. Do you think Mitch and Blanche would have been happily married?
34. Do you feel anger toward any characters?
35. Do you think most people are insecure about aging and losing their beauty?
36. Do you think Stella is naive or totally self-aware?
37. Do you think Blanche feels responsible for ruining her reputation?
38. Do you think Stella should have done more for Blanche?
39. What message(s) are we supposed to take away for ourselves from reading this play?

Personal Response
40. With which character (if any) do you sympathize? Why?
41. Would you recommend this play to a friend? Why or why not?
42. What do you think the girls' mother was like?
43. Would you have liked to have grown up as a sister or brother to Stella and Blanche? Why or why not?
44. What do you think Stanley's father was like?

WRITING ASSIGNMENT #3 - *A Streetcar Named Desire*

PROMPT

Writers write deliberately (even despite students' protestations otherwise!). Authors select words and images to resonate off one another even in different areas of a text. Literary scholars often call this "echoing" another passage. For example, we see Blanche's arrival to the apartment and her departure from it, and these two passages should "echo" or "speak to" one another. Similarly, we see Stanley rapturously embracing Stella twice in the play, and both these moments indicate something to the reader about both Stanley and Stella. You will be examining passages that you believe "echo" one another in your next essay, which will be 4-5 paragraphs in length.

PREWRITING.

Your assignment is to locate three passages from the play which "echo" one another. You should write or type out your passages (a passage is generally 8-20 lines) on a separate sheet and bring that sheet to class next time. Note that you should also think through the connections you see in the passages. You are allowed to make notes about this on your sheet and you should annotate your passages.

DRAFTING

You will have a set amount of time in which to complete this writing assignment. Keep this in mind and budget your time wisely.

Your first paragraph should introduce the commonality that you see in the different passages. For example, your passages may all highlight moments when Blanche feels insecure. Express the connection between the passages as clearly as you can, and perhaps give some background information to support this connection (for example, some reasons why Blanche may be plagued by insecurity).

Your next paragraph should closely analyze the language of your first passage. You should explain the passage, contextualize it, interpret it, and show how it conveys the "connection" you observe. Include relevant quotes from your passage and be sure to explain the quotes as directly as you can. Your next two paragraphs should follow this same model, but should further emphasize the "connection" between the passages and how they "echo" one another.

In your concluding paragraph, restate the "connection" that you have observed and emphasize your main examples. Most importantly, explain the significance of the "connection"–what does it add to our understanding of the novel? Most of your paragraph should be dedicated to proving this significance. One way to think about this is by posing it to yourself as a question: if a reader missed the "connection" that you see, what would he or she fail to understand about the play? Be sure that you have provided adequate textual evidence to support your claims so that you persuade your reader to agree with the significance of your discovery.

A Streetcar Named Desire Writing Assignment #3 Page 2

PROMPT
When you finish the rough draft of your paper, ask a student who sits near you to read it. After reading your rough draft, he/she should tell you what he/she liked best about your work, which parts were difficult to understand, and ways in which your work could be improved. Reread your paper considering your critic's comments, and make the corrections you think are necessary.

PROOFREADING
Do a final proofreading of your paper, double-checking your grammar, spelling, organization, and the clarity of your ideas.

LESSON SIXTEEN

Objectives
1. To practice analytical thinking and persuasive writing
2. To assess student writing
3. To review the vocabulary words from the unit

Activity #1
Use this class time for students to complete Writing Assignment #3 in the amount of time you specify.

Activity #2
Note: If you give your students the entire class period for the writing assignment (or if you wish to orally discuss the ideas students present in their essays in the remaining class time) the following vocabulary review may be done in a separate class period.

When students have completed the in-class writing assignment, they should review the vocabulary from the unit. Choose one (or more) of the vocabulary review activities and spend your class period as directed in the activity. Some of the materials for these review activities are located in the Vocabulary Resource Materials section in this LitPlan.

Activity #3
Give students another vocabulary review activity as homework.

VOCABULARY REVIEW ACTIVITIES

1. Divide your class into two teams and have an old-fashioned spelling or definition bee.

2. Give each of your students (or students in groups of two, three or four) a *Streetcar Named Desire* Vocabulary Word Search Puzzle. The person (group) to find all of the vocabulary words in the puzzle first wins.

3. Give students a *Streetcar Named Desire* Vocabulary Word Search Puzzle without the word list. The person or group to find the most vocabulary words in the puzzle wins.

4. Use a *Streetcar Named Desire* Vocabulary Crossword Puzzle. Put the puzzle onto a transparency on the overhead projector (so everyone can see it), and do the puzzle together as a class.

5. Give students a *Streetcar Named Desire* Vocabulary Matching Worksheet to do.

6. Divide your class into two teams. Use *Streetcar* vocabulary words with their letters jumbled as a word list. Student 1 from Team A faces off against Student 1 from Team B. You write the first jumbled word on the board. The first student (1A or 1B) to unscramble the word wins the chance for his/her team to score points. If 1A wins the jumble, go to student 2A and give him/her a definition. He/she must give you the correct spelling of the vocabulary word which fits that definition. If he/she does, Team A scores a point, and you give student 3A a definition for which you expect a correctly spelled matching vocabulary word. Continue giving Team A definitions until some team member makes an incorrect response. An incorrect response sends the game back to the jumbled-word face off, this time with students 2A and 2B. Instead of repeating giving definitions to the first few students of each team, continue with the student after the one who gave the last incorrect response on the team. For example, if Team B wins the jumbled-word face-off, and student 5B gave the last incorrect answer for Team B, you would start this round of definition questions with student 6B, and so on. The team with the most points wins!

7. Have students write a story in which they correctly use as many vocabulary words as possible. Have students read their compositions orally! Post the most original compositions on your bulletin board!

LESSON SEVENTEEN AND LESSON EIGHTEEN

Objectives
1. To promote creative, analytical thinking
2. To practice writing fiction
3. To gain an awareness for levels of diction
3. To learn how to properly punctuate dialogue

Activity #1
Bring students to a computer lab. Explain to them that they will select a part of a scene (3-4 pages) and convert that scene from drama to fiction.

In order to do this, students should pay attention to the different levels of diction in the play. Contrast the language of the stage directions with the characters' lines of dialogue. Do the words sound the same? Do the passages use the same level of vocabulary? The play's language employs both high and low diction.

Now think about how this would relate to fiction. Descriptions or characters' interior thoughts would likely employ high diction, as would the language of a character like Blanche. Stanley and Mitch, for example, would speak in a lower level of diction.

Emphasize that students can take some creative license as they write, adding details that Williams does not necessarily convey, such as the kind of shoes a character is wearing or what his or her facial expressions looks like. Students should, however, stay close to Williams' plot. Students do not need to include all the dialogue exactly as the characters speak it, but may embellish or condense it accordingly.

Challenge students to use as many vocabulary words from your unit in their writing as possible.

Activity #2
Provide students with a resource on how to incorporate dialogue into fiction. Students are often confused by rules for commas and quotations, as well as when to add returns and line breaks.

Activity #3
Remind students that you will collect their writing at the end of the next class, so they should plan to draft at home as needed.

LESSON NINETEEN

Objectives
1. To share fictional writing assignments
2. To review all of the vocabulary work done in this unit
3. To review unit content in preparation for test

Activity #1
Put students in groups of two. Post a list of the unit vocabulary words on the board. Students should exchange the fictional writing accounts they created in the last two class periods and read them, finding and underlining as many vocabulary words as they can spot.

Activity #2
Collect the compositions and redistribute them at random. Give students time to read their newly acquired papers. Then, ask for volunteers to read any that students think are particularly good. Collect the compositions for grading.

Activity #3
If time permits, select another Vocabulary Review activity from the list provided in Lesson Sixteen.

LESSON TWENTY

Objectives
1. To review the main ideas presented in *A Streetcar Named Desire*
2. To practice asking questions about upcoming tests

Activity #1
Ask students to complete one of the following statements in their journals, logs, or notes.

> One thing that makes me confused about this play is . . .
> One thing that makes me angry about this play is . . .
> One thing that makes me delighted about this play is . . .
> One thing that makes me curious about this play is . . .

Ask students to share their reflections. This is an excellent point of departure for a test review/unit wrap up discussion.

Activity #2
Choose one of the review games/activities included in the packet and follow those detailed directions.

Activity #3
Remind students that the Unit Test will be the following class period. Allow students to ask questions about the test format and your expectations for how best to complete types of questions on the test. Advise students how best to prepare for the test and what materials they should review.

REVIEW GAMES/ACTIVITIES *A Streetcar Named Desire*

1. Ask the class to make up a unit test for *A Streetcar Named Desire*. The test should have 4 sections: matching, true/false, short answer, and essay. Students may use 1/2 period to make the test and then swap papers and use the other 1/2 class period to take a test a classmate has devised. (open book) You may want to use the unit test included in this packet or take questions from the students' unit tests to formulate your own test.

2. Take 1/2 period for students to make up true and false questions (including the answers). Collect the papers and divide the class into two teams. Draw a big tic-tac-toe board on the chalk board. Make one team X and one team O. Ask questions to each side, giving each student one turn. If the question is answered correctly, that students' team's letter (X or O) is placed in the box. If the answer is incorrect, no letter is placed in the box. The object is to get three in a row like tic-tac-toe. You may want to keep track of the number of games won for each team.

3. Take 1/2 period for students to make up questions (true/false and short answer). Collect the questions. Divide the class into two teams. You'll alternate asking questions to individual members of teams A & B (like in a spelling bee). The question keeps going from A to B until it is correctly answered, then a new question is asked. A correct answer does not allow the team to get another question. Correct answers are +2 points; incorrect answers are -1 point.

4. Have students pair up and quiz each other from their study guides and class notes.

5. Give students an *A Streetcar Named Desire* crossword puzzle to complete.

6. Divide your class into two teams. Use *A Streetcar Named Desire* crossword words with their letters jumbled as a word list. Student 1 from Team A faces off against Student 1 from Team B. You write the first jumbled word on the board. The first student (1A or 1B) to unscramble the word wins the chance for his/her team to score points. If 1A wins the jumble, go to student 2A and give him/her a clue. He/she must give you the correct word which matches that clue. If he/she does, Team A scores a point, and you give student 3A a clue for which you expect another correct response. Continue giving Team A clues until some team member makes an incorrect response. An incorrect response sends the game back to the jumbled-word face off, this time with students 2A and 2B. Instead of repeating giving clues to the first few students of each team, continue with the student after the one who gave the last incorrect response on the team. For example, if Team B wins the jumbled-word face-off, and student 5B gave the last incorrect answer for Team B, you would start this round of clue questions with student 6B, and so on. The team with the most points wins!

Review Games Page 2

8. Play What's My Line?. This is similar to the old television show. Students assume the roles of different characters from the epic. One student gives clues to the class, or to a panel of contestants. The contestants try to guess the identity of the guest. Students may enjoy assisting you in creating rules and procedures for the game.

9. Play Jeopardy. Divide the class into two groups. Assign each group a category or book from the epic and have them devise answers for that category. Play the game according to the television show procedures.

10. Play Drawing in the Details. This is similar to Pictionary. Divide students into teams. A student from one team draws a scene from the epic. (You may want to specify the Book or section.) Drawings should be kept simple, to keep the pace lively. Students in the opposing team locate the scene in their books and read it aloud. If they are incorrect, the illustrator's team has a chance to guess. Involve students in setting up a scoring system and any other necessary rules.

UNIT TESTS

SHORT ANSWER UNIT TEST 1 - *A Streetcar Named Desire*

I. Matching/Identify

_____ 1. Belle Reve   A. Cheap hotel

_____ 2. Four Deuces   B. Stella

_____ 3. Flamingo Arms   C. Proof of real estate ownership

_____ 4. Radio   D. Blanche's first husband

_____ 5. Virgo   E. The "moth"

_____ 6. Napoleonic Code   F. Local tavern

_____ 7. Bathroom   G. Marital division of property

_____ 8. Deed   H. Family plantation

_____ 9. Allan   I. Broken in anger

_____ 10. Mother-to-be   J. Blanche's astrological sign

_____ 11. Birthday gift   K. Blanche's refuge

_____ 12. Pajamas   L. Gift for Mitch

_____ 13. Shep   M. Stanley's astrological sign

_____ 14. Marriage   N. Belong to Stanley

_____ 15. Blanche   O. Bus ticket

_____ 16. Capricorn   P. Cause of death

_____ 17. DuBois   Q. Stella's hope for Mitch

_____ 18. Cigarette case   R. Decided not to marry Blanche

_____ 19. Grapes   S. Unlikely to save Blanche

_____ 20. Mitch   T. Means wood

A Streetcar Named Desire Short Answer Unit Test 1 Page 2

II. Short Answer

1. What directions was Blanche given to Stella's place?

2. What happened to Belle Reve?

3. What does Stella mean when she says she is not in anything that she has a desire to get out of?

4. Blanche tells Stella she can't live with Stanley. Why can't she?

5. What does Blanche say about Stanley when she speaks "plainly" about him?

A Streetcar Named Desire Short Answer Unit Test 1 Page 3

6. Who is Shaw? Why is he important in the play?

7. What does Blanche do to the newspaper boy?

8. What does Blanche reveal about her husband?

9. According to Stanley, why did Blanche leave her teaching job at the school?

10. On the night Stanley returns from the hospital, he and Blanche are alone. What happens?

A Streetcar Named Desire Short Answer Unit Test 1 Page 4

III. Essay

Two of the main themes in the play are responsibility and culpability. Responsibility means being aware of the actions that one should take and taking those actions. Culpability is blame for when one fails to take the right actions.

Select one character and explain his or her level of awareness of both his or her responsibilities and culpabilities. In other words, does the character demonstrate an awareness of "right" and "wrong," and what is the significance of his or her awareness or lack of it?

A Streetcar Named Desire Short Answer Unit Test 1 Page 5

IV. Vocabulary: Listen to the vocabulary words and spell them. After you have spelled all the words, go back and write down the definitions.

	Word	Definition
1		
2		
3		
4		
5		
6		
7		
8		
9		
10		

SHORT ANSWER UNIT TEST 1 ANSWER KEY - *A Streetcar Named Desire*

I. Matching/Identify

1. H
2. F
3. A
4. I
5. J
6. G
7. K
8. C
9. D
10. B
11. O
12. N
13. S
14. Q
15. E
16. M
17. T
18. L
19. P
20. R

II. Short Answer

1. What directions was Blanche given to Stella's place?
    Seh was told to take a street-car named Desire, then transfer to one called Cemeteries, and ride six blocks and get off at Elysian Fields.

2. What happened to Belle Reve?
    It was repossessed by the bank.

3. What does Stella mean when she says she is not in anything that she has a desire to get out of?
    She is satisfied by her marriage.

4. Blanche tells Stella she can't live with Stanley. Why can't she?
    She says the only way to live with a man like Stanley is to go to bed with him, and she knows that's Stella's place, not hers.

5. What does Blanche say about Stanley when she speaks "plainly" about him?
    She calls him bestial, animal-like, and ape-like.

6. Who is Shaw? Why is he important in the play?
    He is Stanley's acquaintance who knows Blanche's past. It is from Shaw that Stanley learns about Blanche.

7. What does Blanche do to the newspaper boy?
    She flirts with him, kisses him without his permission, and sends him on his way.

8. What does Blanche reveal about her husband?
    He was homosexual, and he committed suicide.

9. According to Stanley, why did Blanche leave her teaching job at the school?
    She had gotten "mixed-up with" a seventeen-year-old boy and lost her job.

10. On the night Stanley returns from the hospital, he and Blanche are alone. What happens?
    Stanley rapes Blanche.

SHORT ANSWER UNIT TEST 2 - *A Streetcar Named Desire*

I. Matching/Identify

    ____ 1. Birthday gift   A. The "moth"

    ____ 2. Four Deuces   B. Bus ticket

    ____ 3. Flamingo Arms   C. Decided not to marry Blanche

    ____ 4. Virgo   D. Cause of death

    ____ 5. Allan   E. Stanley's astrological sign

    ____ 6. Blanche   F. Family plantation

    ____ 7. Grapes   G. Gift for Mitch

    ____ 8. Deed   H. Means Wood

    ____ 9. Mitch   I. Local tavern

    ____ 10. Mother-to-be   J. Blanche's first husband

    ____ 11. Belle Reve   K. Broken in anger

    ____ 12. Capricorn   L. Proof of real estate ownership

    ____ 13. Shep   M. Blanche's astrological sign

    ____ 14. Napoleonic Code   N. Belong to Stanley

    ____ 15. Pajamas   O. Blanche's refuge

    ____ 16. Radio   P. Cheap hotel

    ____ 17. BuBois   Q. Marital division of property

    ____ 18. Cigarette case   R. Stella

    ____ 19. Marriage   S. Stella's hope for Mitch

    ____ 20. Bathroom   T. Unlikely to save Blanche

A Streetcar Named Desire Short Answer Unit Test 2 Page 2

II. Short Answer

1. How does Blanche feel about Stella's home?

2. Why do Blanche and Stella go out on poker night?

3. What does Blanche say about "soft people"?

4. Why does Blanche want to deceive Mitch?

5. To whom does "pair of queens" refer?

A Streetcar Named Desire Short Answer Unit Test 2 Page 3

6. What does Stanley give Blanche as a birthday present?

7. Why does Mitch ask Blanche if she is out of her mind?

8. Where is Stella sending Blanche in the final scene of the play?

9. What advice does Eunice give Stella?

11. On what does Blanche say she has always depended?

A Streetcar Named Desire Short Answer Unit Test 2 Page 4

III. Composition

Carefully read the quote from the play below. It occurs in Scene 10, as Stanley carries Blanche to the bed:

"We've had this date with each other from the beginning."

Explain the statement, focusing on Stanley's emphasis on inevitability.

A Streetcar Named Desire Short Answer Unit Test 2 Page 5

IV. Vocabulary: Listen to the vocabulary words and spell them. After you have spelled all the words, go back and write down the definitions.

	Word	Definition
1		
2		
3		
4		
5		
6		
7		
8		
9		
10		

ANSWER KEY: SHORT ANSWER UNIT TEST 2 - *A Streetcar Named Desire*

I. Matching/Identify

1. B
2. I
3. P
4. M
5. J
6. A
7. D
8. L
9. C
10. R
11. F
12. E
13. T
14. Q
15. N
16. K
17. H
18. G
19. S
20. O

II. Short Answer

1. How does Blanche feel about Stella's home?
   She says only Edgar Allan Poe could do it justice, and she asks why Stella never told her that she has to live in "these conditions."

2. Why do Blanche and Stella go out on poker night?
   They are not invited when the men are playing poker.

3. What does Blanche say about "soft people"?
   She says "soft people have to shimmer and glow. . . . It isn't enough to be soft. You've got to be soft and attractive."

4. Why does Blanche want to deceive Mitch?
   She wants to deceive him enough to make him want her.

5. To whom does "pair of queens" refer?
   It refers to Stella and Blanche.

6. What does Stanley give Blanche as a birthday present?
   He gives Blanche a bus ticket.

7. Why does Mitch ask Blanche if she is out of her mind?
   Blanche is talking about music that isn't playing and "the shot." She is somehow re-living the evening her husband killed himself.

8. Where is Stella sending Blanche in the final scene of the play?
   Stella is sending Blanche to an asylum.

9. What advice does Eunice give Stella?
   "Life has to go on. No matter what happens, you have to keep on going."

11. On what does Blanche say she has always depended?
    Blanche says she has always depended on the kindness of strangers.

ADVANCED SHORT ANSWER UNIT TEST - *A Streetcar Named Desire*

I. Matching/Identify

____ 1. Birthday gift   A. The "moth"

____ 2. Four Deuces   B. Bus ticket

____ 3. Flamingo Arms   C. Decided not to marry Blanche

____ 4. Virgo   D. Cause of death

____ 5. Shaw   E. Stanley's astrological sign

____ 6. Blanche   F. Family plantation

____ 7. Grapes   G. Gift for Mitch

____ 8. Deed   H. Means wood

____ 9. Mitch   I. Local tavern

____ 10. Mother-to-be   J. Told Stanley about Blanche's past

____ 11. Belle Reve   K. Broken in anger

____ 12. Capricorn   L. Proof of real estate ownership

____ 13. Shep   M. Blanche's astrological sign

____ 14. Napoleonic Code   N. Blanche's profession

____ 15. Teacher   O. Blanche's refuge

____ 16. Radio   P. Cheap hotel

____ 17. DuBois   Q. Marital division of property

____ 18. Cigarette case   R. Stella

____ 19. Marriage   S. Stella's hope for Mitch

____ 20. Bathroom   T. Unlikely to save Blanche

A Streetcar Named Desire Advanced Short Answer Unit Test Page 2

II. Short Answer

1. One of the concepts explored by the play is marriage, as we see Steve and Eunice, Stanley and Stella, Allan and Blanche, and potentially Mitch and Blanche. How, ultimately, is marriage portrayed in the play?

2. How does the setting contribute to the meaning of the play?

A Streetcar Named Desire Advanced Short Answer Unit Test Page 3

3. What does Blanche's interaction with the paperboy reveal about her?

4. Is Stella a victim? Why or why not?

5. Are Stanley and Blanche more alike or dissimilar? Explain.

A Streetcar Named Desire Advanced Short Answer Unit Test Page 4

III. Quotations: Identify the speaker and discuss the significance of each quotation.

1. "Nobody's going to get up, so don't be worried."

2. "I loved someone, too, and the person I loved I lost."

3. "What it means is I've never had a real good look at you, Blanche. Let's turn the light on here."

A Streetcar Named Desire Advanced Short Answer Unit Test Page 5

4. "It's always a powder-keg. He didn't know what he was doing . . . He was as good as a lamb when I came back and he's really very, very ashamed of himself."

5. "Whoever you are–I have always depended on the kindness of strangers."

6. "You make my mouth water."

A Streetcar Named Desire Advanced Short Answer Unit Test Page 6

7. "I know, I know. But you are the one that abandoned Belle Reve, not I! I stayed and fought for it, bled for it, almost died for it!"

8. "Now let's have a gander at the bill of sale."

9. "The Kowalskis and the DuBois have different notions."

10. "How about taking a swim, a moonlight swim at the old rock quarry? If anyone's sober enough to drive a car?"

A Streetcar Named Desire Advanced Short Answer Unit Test Page 7

III. Vocabulary: Write down the vocabulary words given, then write a paragraph or two about *Streetcar* correctly using ten of the words.

1.	5.	9.
2.	6.	10.
3.	7.	11.
4.	8.	12.

ANSWER KEY: ADVANCED SHORT ANSWER UNIT TEST

I. Matching/Identify

1. B
2. I
3. P
4. M
5. J
6. A
7. D
8. L
9. C
10. R
11. F
12. E
13. T
14. Q
15. N
16. K
17. H
18. G
19. S
20. O

II. Short Answer: Answers will vary with the level of class discussion.

III. Quotations: Identify the speaker and discuss the significance of each quotation.

1. "Nobody's going to get up, so don't be worried."

    Stanley says this in response to Blanche who, upon meeting Stanley's friends, says "Please don't get up." This emphasizes the difference in class between Blanche and Stanley, as symbolized by the lack of gentility and courtesy, to which Blanche is accustomed. The lack of chivalry extended to Blanche suggests that she may not be a lady worthy of it.

2. "I loved someone, too, and the person I loved I lost."

    Blanche confides in Mitch about her husband, who committed suicide when Blanche learned of his infidelities with men. For Blanche, her feelings of true love and security were replaced with loss and loneliness.

3. "What it means is I've never had a real good look at you, Blanche. Let's turn the light on here."

As Mitch becomes more serious in his intentions toward a possible marriage to Blanche, he wishes to see her in brighter light, as he has never seen her in daylight. The light motif is related to Blanche's propensity for lying to Mitch and misleading him. He is attempting to "illuminate" the truth about her.

4. "It's always a powder-keg. He didn't know what he was doing . . . He was as good as a lamb when I came back and he's really very, very ashamed of himself."

Stella attempts to explain to Blanche why she has reconciled with Stanley despite the fact that he struck her. The word "lamb" echoes with the word "wolf" which was applied to Stanley earlier in the play–as if he has an insatiable appetite which leads to his uneven tendencies toward abuse. Stella may need to say this to convince herself of making an acceptable choice.

5. "Whoever you are–I have always depended on the kindness of strangers."

Blanche does not recognize or understand who the doctor and nurse are who are transporting her to an asylum. Here Blanche states what has been the proclivity of her character: she does not accept responsibility for her situation, but to rely on how others view her and her skills for manipulating them.

6. "You make my mouth water."

Blanche says this, rather inappropriately, to the newspaper boy. After unsuccessfully attempting to seduce him, she becomes more manifest in her language, eschewing innuendo and being very direct about sexually propositioning the young man. The dialogue suggests Blanche as similarly voracious sexually as Stanley.

7. "I know, I know. But you are the one that abandoned Belle Reve, not I! I stayed and fought for it, bled for it, almost died for it!"

Blanche is appealing to Stella for sympathy in the loss of Belle Reve and the role Blanche has played in their family as caretaker. Though Stella is unaware of Blanche's recent past, Blanche is also attempting to receive dispensation for her questionably moral behaviors.

8. "Now let's have a gander at the bill of sale."

Stanley says this to Stella as he presses her to believe that Blanche has profited from a transaction of the Belle Reve property. This shows his animosity toward Blanche, as well as the same materialism and entitlement which he criticizes in her.

9. "The Kowalskis and the DuBois have different notions."

Stanley says this to delineate the differences in class expectations between Blanche and himself. This line is especially important because it creates a divide between Stanley and Stella, and exposes the conflict within Stella herself who is both Kowalski and DuBois.

10. "How about taking a swim, a moonlight swim at the old rock quarry? If anyone's sober enough to drive a car?"

Blanche has lost touch with the distinction between illusion and reality. Here she prefers to live in the past rather than face the problems of her present. The line also points to Blanche's increasing dependence on alcohol and how it is contributing to her quick demise.

MULTIPLE CHOICE UNIT TEST 1 - *A Streetcar Named Desire*

I. Matching/Identify

____ 1. Belle Reve   A. Cheap hotel

____ 2. Four Deuces   B. Stella

____ 3. Flamingo Arms   C. Proof of real estate ownership

____ 4. Radio   D. Blanche's first husband

____ 5. Virgo   E. The "moth"

____ 6. Napoleonic Code   F. Local tavern

____ 7. Bathroom   G. Marital division of property

____ 8. Deed   H. Family plantation

____ 9. Allan   I. Broken in anger

____ 10. Mother-to-be   J. Blanche's astrological sign

____ 11. Birthday gift   K. Blanche's refuge

____ 12. Pajamas   L. Gift for Mitch

____ 13. Shep   M. Stanley's astrological sign

____ 14. Marriage   N. Belong to Stanley

____ 15. Blanche   O. Bus ticket

____ 16. Capricorn   P. Cause of death

____ 17. DuBois   Q. Stella's hope for Mitch

____ 18. Cigarette case   R. Decided not to marry Blanche

____ 19. Grapes   S. Unlikely to save Blanche

____ 20. Mitch   T. Means wood

A Streetcar Named Desire Multiple Choice Unit Test 1 Page 2

II. Multiple Choice

1. What job did Blanche previously have?
     A. Social worker
     B. Secretary
     C. Teacher
     D. Prostitute

2. What happened to Belle Reve?
     A. It was destroyed.
     B. It was repossessed by the bank.
     C. It was sold by Blanche.
     D. It was spilled.

3. What does Blanche say she'll burn?
     A. The deed to Belle Reve
     B. Love letters that Stanley has touched
     C. The dress she traveled in
     D. A book of poems

4. What was Stella's response to Stanley's breaking the light bulbs on their wedding night?
     A. Felt happy
     B. Felt angry
     C. Felt ignored
     D. Felt excited

5. Who is Shaw?
     A. Blanche's old beau
     B. Shep's cousin
     C. Stanley's acquaintance
     D. Drugstore clerk

6. What does Blanche reveal about her husband?
     A. She killed him.
     B. He was homosexual.
     C. She never loved him.
     D. He asked her for a divorce.

A Streetcar Named Desire Multiple Choice Unit Test 1 Page 3

7. How does Stanley make sure that Blanche will leave?
    A. He buys her a bus ticket.
    B. He packs her suitcase.
    C. He forbids her to use the bathroom.
    D. He kicks Stella out too.

8. What does Blanche "rename" the Flamingo?
    A. The Desert Oasis
    B. The Terrible Prison
    C. The Tarantula Arms Hotel
    D. The Little Birdie Motel

9. From whom does Blanche claim she has received a telegram?
    A. Belle Reve
    B. Bill Shaw
    C. The manager of The Flamingo
    D. Shep Huntleigh

10. Where is Stella sending Blanche?
    A. On a vacation to Miami
    B. Aunt Ethel's house
    C. An asylum
    D. Belle Reve

A Streetcar Named Desire Multiple Choice Unit Test 1 Page 4

III. Composition

Select one of the following topics and write a 3-4 paragraph composition that focuses on that topic.

1. Select one of the following motifs and explain its significance to the overall meaning of the play: poker, grooming, light, or music.

2. People can often be said to be influenced–haunted even–by their pasts. Select from Stanley, Mitch, or Blanche and explain how the past affects that character.

3. The play considers relationships and what makes those relationships successful. Consider spouse or sibling relationships in the play. Select one and explain how it is or is not successful.

A Streetcar Named Desire Multiple Choice Unit Test 1 Page 5

IV. Vocabulary - Match the correct definitions to the words.

____ 1. raffish   A. calmly

____ 2. reproach   B. criticizing

____ 3. swindled   C. showy

____ 4. improvident   D. overly sweet

____ 5. lurid   E. unpredictable; not consistent

____ 6. feigned   F. crude; rough; unpolished

____ 7. gaudy   G. foolish talk

____ 8. bestial   H. vulgar

____ 9. prim   I. pretended

____ 10. temperamental   J. scam

____ 11. reproving   K. blame

____ 12. affectation   L. friendliness

____ 13. saccharine   M. poor; without necesities

____ 14. serenely   N. fakeness

____ 15. amiability   O. inhuman

____ 16. uncouth   P. lacking judgment

____ 17. malarkey   Q. unable to move or act

____ 18. destitute   R. stiffly proper or precise in manner or appearance

____ 19. inert   S. horrible

____ 20. elated   T. happy

MULTIPLE CHOICE UNIT TEST 2 - *A Streetcar Named Desire*

I. Matching/Identify

____ 1. Birthday gift   A. The "moth"

____ 2. Four Deuces   B. Bus ticket

____ 3. Flamingo Arms   C. Decided not to marry Blanche

____ 4. Virgo   D. Cause of death

____ 5. Shaw   E. Stanley's astrological sign

____ 6. Blanche   F. Family plantation

____ 7. Grapes   G. Gift for Mitch

____ 8. Deed   H. Means wood

____ 9. Mitch   I. Local tavern

____ 10. Mother-to-be   J. Told Stanley about Blanche's past

____ 11. Belle Reve   K. Broken in anger

____ 12. Capricorn   L. Proof of real estate ownership

____ 13. Shep   M. Blanche's astrological sign

____ 14. Napoleonic Code   N. Blanche's profession

____ 15. Teacher   O. Blanche's refuge

____ 16. Radio   P. Cheap hotel

____ 17. DuBois   Q. Marital division of property

____ 18. Cigarette case   R. Stella

____ 19. Marriage   S. Stella's hope for Mitch

____ 20. Bathroom   T. Unlikely to save Blanche

A Streetcar Named Desire Multiple Choice Unit Test 2 Page 2

II. Multiple Choice

1. What happens to Belle Reve?
    A. It is repossessed.
    B. Blanche donates it.
    C. Stanley inherits it.
    D. It is burned in a fire.

2. Why does Blanche say she left her job?
    A. Her nerves broke.
    B. She was fired.
    C. She was bored.
    D. Her patience was exhausted.

3. What, according to Stella, is Blanche's weakness?
    A. Her appearance
    B. Her intelligence
    C. Her lack of a husband
    D. Her need for attention

4. What does Stanley say the Napoleonic Code is?
    A. Spousal ownership of property
    B. Conquering territory in France
    C. Husbands own all property
    D. Unconditional honesty

5. For what does Blanche thank Mitch?
    A. A bouquet of carnations
    B. A bottle of wine
    C. Kindness
    D. Money he loaned her

6. With what does Blanche threaten Stanley?
    A. Yelling fire
    B. A broken bottle
    C. Telling Stella about their affair
    D. Not sharing the profits from Belle Reve

7. Why does Mitch no longer want to marry Blanche?
    A. He says she is not clean.
    B. He thinks she is too young.
    C. He thinks she is too old.
    D. His old girlfriend has come back to him.

A Streetcar Named Desire Multiple Choice Unit Test 2 Page 3

8. What will make Blanche "weep with joy"?
    A. Reuniting with Shep
    B. Leaving and having privacy again
    C. Having a niece or nephew
    D. Being told she is beautiful

9. What advice does Eunice give Stella?
    A. Divorce Stanley before it is too late.
    B. No matter what happens, you have to keep on going.
    C. Disown Blanche entirely and don't have any regrets.
    D. Take the baby and go to a women's shelter.

10. On what does Blanche say she has always depended?
    A. The kindness of strangers
    B. Her stunning good looks
    C. Her ability to seduce
    D. Her good reputation

A Streetcar Named Desire Multiple Choice Unit Test 2 Page 4

III. Composition: Choose ONE of these topics and write a complete essay.

1. One of the primary conflicts in this play is illusion versus reality. Select a character from the play and explain how the character is conflicted between the two: does he or she embrace reality or illusion?

2. Explain how feelings of loneliness or abandonment cause vulnerability in two of the following characters: Stella, Mitch, Stanley, or Blanche. Explain what the two characters have in common.

A Streetcar Named Desire Multiple Choice Unit Test 2 Page 5

IV. Vocabulary - Match the correct definitions to the words.

____ 1. raffish   A. calmly

____ 2. reproach   B. blame

____ 3. swindled   C. showy

____ 4. improvident   D. overly sweet

____ 5. lurid   E. unpredictable; not consistant

____ 6. feigned   F. crude; rough; unpolished

____ 7. gaudy   G. foolish talk

____ 8. bestial   H. vulgar

____ 9. prim   I. pretended

____ 10. temperamental   J. scam

____ 11. reproving   K. criticizing

____ 12. affectation   L. friendliness

____ 13. saccharine   M. poor; without necessities

____ 14. serenely   N. fakeness

____ 15. amiability   O. inhuman

____ 16. uncouth   P. lacking judgment

____ 17. malarkey   Q. unable to move or act

____ 18. destitute   R. stiffly proper or precise in manner or appearance

____ 19. inert   S. horrible

____ 20. elated   T. happy

ANSWER SHEET - *A Streetcar Named Desire*
Multiple Choice Unit Tests

I. Matching	II. Multiple Choice	IV. Vocabulary
1. ___	1. ___	1. ___
2. ___	2. ___	2. ___
3. ___	3. ___	3. ___
4. ___	4. ___	4. ___
5. ___	5. ___	5. ___
6. ___	6. ___	6. ___
7. ___	7. ___	7. ___
8. ___	8. ___	8. ___
9. ___	9. ___	9. ___
10. ___	10. ___	10. ___
11. ___	11. ___	11. ___
12. ___	12. ___	12. ___
13. ___	13. ___	13. ___
14. ___	14. ___	14. ___
15. ___	15. ___	15. ___
16. ___	16. ___	16. ___
17. ___	17. ___	17. ___
18. ___	18. ___	18. ___
19. ___	19. ___	19. ___
20. ___	20. ___	20. ___

ANSWER KEY - *A Streetcar Named Desire*
Multiple Choice Unit Test 1

I. Matching	II. Multiple Choice	IV. Vocabulary
1. H	1. C	1. H
2. F	2. B	2. K
3. A	3. B	3. J
4. I	4. D	4. P
5. J	5. C	5. S
6. G	6. B	6. I
7. K	7. A	7. C
8. C	8. C	8. O
9. D	9. D	9. R
10. B	10. C	10. E
11. O		11. B
12. N		12. N
13. S		13. D
14. Q		14. A
15. E		15. L
16. M		16. F
17. T		17. G
18. L		18. M
19. P		19. Q
20. R		20. T

ANSWER KEY - *A Streetcar Named Desire*
Multiple Choice Unit Test 2

I. Matching	II. Multiple Choice	IV. Vocabulary
1. B	1. A	1. H
2. I	2. A	2. B
3. P	3. A	3. J
4. M	4. A	4. P
5. J	5. C	5. S
6. A	6. B	6. I
7. D	7. A	7. C
8. L	8. B	8. O
9. C	9. B	9. R
10. R	10. A	10. E
11. F		11. K
12. E		12. N
13. T		13. D
14. Q		14. A
15. N		15. L
16. K		16. F
17. H		17. G
18. G		18. M
19. S		19. Q
20. O		20. T

UNIT RESOURCE MATERIALS

BULLETIN BOARD IDEAS - *A Streetcar Named Desire*

1. Save one corner of the board for the best of students' *A Streetcar Named Desire* writing assignments.

2. Take one of the word search puzzles from the extra activities packet and with a marker copy it over in a large size on the bulletin board. Write the clue words to find to one side. Invite students prior to and after class to find the words and circle them on the bulletin board.

3. Write several of the most significant quotations from the book onto the board on brightly colored paper.

4. Make a bulletin board listing the vocabulary words for this unit. As you complete sections of the novel and discuss the vocabulary for each section, write the definitions on the bulletin board. (If your board is one students face frequently, it will help them learn the words.)

5. Have students look through magazines for pictures of people who resemble the descriptions of main characters. Clip out the pictures and hang them on the bulletin board with quotes about the characters.

6. Have students make copies of the Non-fiction articles they read and hang them on the board with a push pin to create a lending library of articles related to the novel.

7. Find pictures of New Orleans and articles about the history of the city and post those on the board.

8. Research other plays that were later made into films. Title the bulletin board Page to Screen and add summaries of the plays, copies of the corresponding book covers, and film stills from the film.

9. Title your bulletin board What's Better, the Book or the Movie? and have each student find 2 people to interview, asking the interviewee to think of a book or movie that he or she enjoyed more than its book or movie counterpart. On a 3"x5" card, record the title of the book or film and the interviewee's opinion. Hang these on the bulletin board.

10. The play has several references to music, both polka and jazz. Research musicians, especially musicians from the New Orleans area, and post their pictures, biographies and discographies on the bulletin board.

EXTRA ACTIVITIES - *A Streetcar Named Desire*

One of the difficulties in teaching a work of literature is that all students don't read or synthesize material at the same speed. One student who likes to read may take the book home and finish it in a day or two. Sometimes a few students finish the in-class assignments early. The problem, then, is finding suitable extra activities for students.

One thing that seems to help is to keep a little library in the classroom. For this unit on *A Streetcar Named Desire*, you might check out from the school library other plays by Tennessee Williams, including *Cat on a Hot Tin Roof, The Glass Menagerie,* and *Night of the Iguana.* Your library may have excellent anthologies of short American drama from the mid-twentieth century as well. Consider adding articles or books about mental illness, family relationships, tips for successful relationships or marriages, New Orleans, laws regarding gambling and poker, famous poker players, prenatal care, life on a southern plantation, abuse hotlines, rape, violence, or careers in counseling.

Some students may like to draw. You might devise a contest or allow some extra-credit grade for students who draw characters or scenes from *A Streetcar Named Desire.* Note, too, that if the students do not want to keep their drawings you may pick up some extra bulletin board materials this way. If you have a contest and you supply the prize (an iTune download or something like that perhaps), you could, possibly, make the drawing itself a non-returnable entry fee.

If you have a computer in your classroom, students who finish early and are technically inclined might compile a list of websites related to *A Streetcar Named Desire* and create a class resource web page.

Other things you may keep on hand are puzzles. We have made some relating directly to *A Streetcar Named Desire* for you. Feel free to duplicate them for your students to use. Completion of these might result in extra-credit.

The pages which follow contain games, puzzles and worksheets. The keys, when appropriate, immediately follow the puzzle or worksheet. There are two main groups of activities: one group for the unit; that is, generally relating to *A Streetcar Named Desire* text, and another group of activities related strictly to *A Streetcar Named Desire* vocabulary.

Directions for these games, puzzles and worksheets are self-explanatory. The object here is to provide you with extra materials you may use in any way you choose.

MORE ACTIVITIES - *A Streetcar Named Desire*

1. Have students work together to make a time line chronology of the events in the story. Take a large piece of construction paper and on one wall (or however you can physically arrange it in your room) and make the events of the story along it. Students may want to add drawings or cut-out pictures to represent the events (as well as a written statement). The play opens in May and closes in late fall, less than a year later.

2. Have students design a playbill and handbill for *A Streetcar Named Desire.*

3. Have students design a bulletin board (ready to be put up; not just sketched) for *A Streetcar Named Desire.*

4. Have students imagine their ideal "significant others." Have them write a Match.com-type profile for this hypothetical ideal.

5. Have students choose one minor character (Mitch, Eunice, Steve, Pablo, Mexican Woman) and write a scene or one-act play that focuses specifically on that character.

6. Have students assume the persona of a character and write a letter from that character to another.

7. Have students learn about the diversity of New Orleans by investigating art, architecture, music or cuisine. Students should focus on the different cultural influences (Creole, French, African American, etc.) that relate to the region's art, architecture, music or cuisine.

8. Have students write a "lost scene" in which Mitch introduces Blanche to his mother.

9. Two of the play's motifs are games: bowling and poker. Learn the rules for these games and possibly play them.

10. Research the allusions in the novel. Define them and create a reference guide for next year's class.

11. Learn about home ownership and repossession. Invite a real estate agent to speak to the class about the basics of home ownership.

More Activities *A Streetcar Named Desire* Continued

12. Have students write descriptions of their dream homes. Using the newspaper and internet as resources, students can "buy" their real dream homes.

13. Create a class website that includes student writing and links to resources.

14. Invite an alcohol awareness expert to talk to the class about the signs of alcoholism and the disease itself.

15. Have students research the process of grieving, such as the work by Elisabeth Kubler Ross.

16. Have students research the history of streetcars in America. In conjunction, have students learn about public transportation in their town. Students might also design public transportation systems for their neighborhoods.

17. Have students research historical preservation of grand Southern plantations.

18. The film version of *A Streetcar Named Desire* may be a useful teaching tool. The film's dialogue does differ from the exact text of the play. Students might "read along" with the film, making notations of these departures.

19. An episode of *The Simpsons* parodies the play. Students might view the episode, learn about parody and write a parody of a simple story such as a fairytale or legend.

20. The play is frequently produce. See if your class might attend a local performance. If time and funds do not permit, perhaps a cast member can visit your class.

21. Have a debate about the roles of men and women in marriage, or society in general.

22. Students can create a map or diorama of the play's settings, including Elysian Fields, The Four Deuces, Lake Pontchartrain and so on, including major New Orleans landmarks.

23. Write a memoir from "Baby" Kowalski's perspective. Imagine what she would write about growing up with her parents.

More Activities *A Streetcar Named Desire* Continued

24. Have students discover the meaning of their names.

25. Write a flashback scene featuring Blanche and Allan.

26. Have small groups act out scenes, complete with props and sets.

27. Have students write about a time when they were confronted with a difficult choice.

28. Have students write love letters to "young" Blanche or to a recipient of their choice.

29. Have students learn about Southern literary traditions and identify a list of ten influential Southern writers.

A Streetcar Named Desire Word List

No.	Word	Clue/Definition
1.	ALLAN	He took his own life.
2.	APPEARANCE	According to Stella, this is Blanche's weakness.
3.	ARMS	Blanche renames the Flamingo The Tarantula ___ Hotel.
4.	ASYLUM	Blanche's destination
5.	BELLE	Lost plantation: ___ Reve
6.	BLANCHE	She ends up being sent to an institution.
7.	BOTTLE	Blanche physically threatens Stanley with a broken one.
8.	BUTTONS	Blanche asks Stanley for help with these.
9.	CIGARETTE	Mitch's ___ case was from a former girlfriend.
10.	CODE	Stanley says spousal ownership of property is the Napoleonic ___. In
11.	CORN	Stanley's joke, the rooster stopped pursuing the hen because of this.
12.	DEED	Proves home ownership
13.	ELYSIAN	Ironic apartment name; ___ Fields
14.	EUNICE	She accuses Steve of having an affair.
15.	FIRE	The word Blanche screams
16.	FLAMINGO	Cheap hotel of ill repute from which Blanche was asked to leave The
17.	FLOWERS	Mexican woman sells these.
18.	GRAPES	Blanche says eating unwashed ___ will cause her to die.
19.	HAROLD	Mitch's real name
20.	HOSPITAL	Stella is rushed there.
21.	ILLUSION	A woman's charm is fifty percent this.
22.	LANTERN	Stanley asks Blanche if she wants to take her paper one with her.
23.	LEAVING	It would make Blanche weep with joy.
24.	LETTERS	Blanche says she'll burn these that Stanley has touched.
25.	LIFE	According to Eunice, it keeps on going.
26.	LIGHTBULBS	Stanley smashed these on the wedding night.
27.	MITCH	He dumped Blanche when he found out about her past.
28.	MOTH	Williams compares Blanche's manner and clothing to this.
29.	MUSIC	Blanche hears this, which is not actually playing.
30.	PIG	Stella calls Stanley a ___.
31.	PLEIADES	Blanche seeks this in the sky.
32.	POE	Blanche says only he could describe the Kowalskis' living conditions.
33.	POKER	Game Stanley and the men played
34.	POLISH	Stanley's ethnic heritage
35.	PREGNANT	Stella's condition
36.	QUEENS	Stella and Blanche are referred to as a pair of ___.
37.	RADIO	Stanley threw it out the window.
38.	RHINESTONES	False gems
39.	SETTING	New Orleans
40.	SHAW	He knows the gossip about Blanche.
41.	SHEP	Blanche said he sent a telegram.
42.	SILK	Wedding night pajamas were made of this
43.	STANLEY	He rapes Blanche.
44.	STELLA	Blanche's sister; Stanley's wife
45.	STRANGERS	Blanche depended on the kindness of ___.
46.	STREETCAR	It is named Desire.

A Streetcar Named Desire Word List Continued

No. Word	Clue/Definition
47. TIARA	At the start of Scene 10, Blanche wears a white evening gown, slippers, and this.
48. TICKET	Stanley buys Blanche one for her birthday.
49. VIRGO	Blanche's astrological sign
50. WHITE	Meaning of Blanche's name
51. WILLIAMS	Author Tennessee
52. WOOD	The name DuBois means this.

WORD SEARCH - A Streetcar Named Desire

```
P S E T T I N G F L A M I N G O P L S N
I H R L R H Q Q D W H I T E B G L V T B
G N M A F S P F J E N M L L R E T R V
V O D P Z I Y R V R E J J Y I I I J E T
S I L K F L O W E R S D G S G V A S E D
O S G Q K O E T B G H K L I H L D T T R
D U C S C P N T A U N Z S A T H E A C B
W L F X M A Y E T S T A K N B X S N A B
L N W L Y M T F E Y T N V U S Y L R H
E I H O S P I T A L R L O T L A V E L G
A H T V Q U E E N S T S U N B R D Y B S
V G I E T Z M R B C A C B M S M P B D L
I C C N U W U A E J L D F R A S O O L T
N Q K Q H N S G L W L P E T L G O T E S
G S E C X N I I L P A G P I L W D H H G
B O T T L E C C E C N A R A E P P A L W
H I G R S O J H E A O Y D R T O W R I F
M F Y C R H S B R N P D I A S K Y O F Q
B L A N C H E T Y R Z F E M M E H L E F
W R H I N E S T O N E S E P A R G D D X
```

ALLAN	DEED	LEAVING	POLISH	STRANGERS
APPEARANCE	ELYSIAN	LETTERS	PREGNANT	STREETCAR
ARMS	EUNICE	LIFE	QUEENS	TIARA
ASYLUM	FIRE	LIGHTBULBS	RADIO	TICKET
BELLE	FLAMINGO	MITCH	RHINESTONES	VIRGO
BLANCHE	FLOWERS	MOTH	SETTING	WHITE
BOTTLE	GRAPES	MUSIC	SHAW	WOOD
BUTTONS	HAROLD	PIG	SHEP	
CIGARETTE	HOSPITAL	PLEIADES	SILK	
CODE	ILLUSION	POE	STANLEY	
CORN	LANTERN	POKER	STELLA	

WORD SEARCH ANSWER KEY - A Streetcar Named Desire

```
P S E T T I N G F L A M I N G O P       S
I     R H     D W H I T E     G L       T
G  N  A  S P    E N      L L  R E       R
   O D   I  R   R E      Y I  I         E
S I L K F L O W E R S D  S G  A         E
O  S     O  T B G        I H  D T       T
U        P  N A U N      A T  E A       C
L        A  E S T        N B  S N       A
L  L     L  T Y N        U    L L       R
E I H O S P I T A L R  L O T  A E       
  T   Q U E E N S   S U N B R Y         
V I     E   M R B   A     M S M P       D
I   C   U   U A E   L     R A S O       O
N   K   H   N S G L L E T L L O T E     S
G   E   C   I I L P A G   I W H H L
B O T T L E C C E N A R A E P P A       L
    I       O   H E A O   R T O W R     I
M           R   S R   D I A S K O       F
B L A N C H E T       F E     E L       E
R H I N E S T O N E S E P A R G D
```

ALLAN	DEED	LEAVING	POLISH	STRANGERS
APPEARANCE	ELYSIAN	LETTERS	PREGNANT	STREETCAR
ARMS	EUNICE	LIFE	QUEENS	TIARA
ASYLUM	FIRE	LIGHTBULBS	RADIO	TICKET
BELLE	FLAMINGO	MITCH	RHINESTONES	VIRGO
BLANCHE	FLOWERS	MOTH	SETTING	WHITE
BOTTLE	GRAPES	MUSIC	SHAW	WOOD
BUTTONS	HAROLD	PIG	SHEP	
CIGARETTE	HOSPITAL	PLEIADES	SILK	
CODE	ILLUSION	POE	STANLEY	
CORN	LANTERN	POKER	STELLA	

CROSSWORD - A Streetcar Named Desire

Across

2. Mitch's ____ case was from a former girlfriend.
5. Cheap hotel of ill repute from which Blanche was asked to leave
7. Stanley says spousal ownership of property is the Napoleonic ___.
8. Lost plantation: ___ Reve
9. The Mexican woman sells these.
13. He dumped Blanche when he found out about her past.
15. Stella calls Stanley a ___.
16. Meaning of Blanche's name
18. Blanche asks Stanley for help with these.
19. Blanche hears this, which is not actually playing.
20. According to Eunice, it keeps on going.
21. Blanche physically threatens Stanley with a broken one.
22. Stella is rushed there.

Down

1. Wedding night pajamas were made of this
2. In Stanley's joke, the rooster stopped pursuing the hen because of this.
3. Stanley threw it out the window.
4. Stanley buys Blanche one for her birthday.
5. The word Blanche screams
6. Blanche's destination
8. She ends up being sent to an institution.
10. Stanley smashed these on the wedding night.
11. New Orleans
12. He knows the gossip about Blanche.
14. A woman's charm is fifty percent this.
15. Stanley's ethnic heritage
17. Blanche renames the Flamingo The Tarantula ___ Hotel.

CROSSWORD ANSEWR KEY - A Streetcar Named Desire

Across
2. Mitch's ____ case was from a former girlfriend.
5. Cheap hotel of ill repute from which Blanche was asked to leave
7. Stanley says spousal ownership of property is the Napoleonic ___.
8. Lost plantation: ___ Reve
9. The Mexican woman sells these.
13. He dumped Blanche when he found out about her past.
15. Stella calls Stanley a ___.
16. Meaning of Blanche's name
18. Blanche asks Stanley for help with these.
19. Blanche hears this, which is not actually playing.
20. According to Eunice, it keeps on going.
21. Blanche physically threatens Stanley with a broken one.
22. Stella is rushed there.

Down
1. Wedding night pajamas were made of this
2. In Stanley's joke, the rooster stopped pursuing the hen because of this.
3. Stanley threw it out the window.
4. Stanley buys Blanche one for her birthday.
5. The word Blanche screams
6. Blanche's destination
8. She ends up being sent to an institution.
10. Stanley smashed these on the wedding night.
11. New Orleans
12. He knows the gossip about Blanche.
14. A woman's charm is fifty percent this.
15. Stanley's ethnic heritage
17. Blanche renames the Flamingo The Tarantula ___ Hotel.

MATCHING 1 - A Streetcar Named Desire

___ 1. FIRE
___ 2. MUSIC
___ 3. WOOD
___ 4. ILLUSION
___ 5. MITCH
___ 6. SETTING
___ 7. APPEARANCE
___ 8. CIGARETTE
___ 9. POLISH
___ 10. BELLE
___ 11. LANTERN
___ 12. WHITE
___ 13. LIFE
___ 14. ALLAN
___ 15. HOSPITAL
___ 16. TIARA
___ 17. WILLIAMS
___ 18. HAROLD
___ 19. BLANCHE
___ 20. TICKET
___ 21. RADIO
___ 22. SHEP
___ 23. ELYSIAN
___ 24. SILK
___ 25. SHAW

A. Wedding night pajamas were made of this
B. Stanley's ethnic heritage
C. Mitch's ____ case was from a former girlfriend.
D. New Orleans
E. The name DuBois means this.
F. He dumped Blanche when he found out about her past.
G. The word Blanche screams
H. Stanley threw it out the window.
I. Blanche said he sent a telegram.
J. A woman's charm is fifty percent this.
K. Mitch's real name
L. Ironic apartment name; ___ Fields
M. Author
N. Stanley asks Blanche if she wants to take her paper one with her.
O. He knows the gossip about Blanche.
P. At the start of Scene 10 Blanche wears a white evening gown, slippers, and this.
Q. She ends up being sent to an institution.
R. Stanley buys Blanche one for her birthday.
S. Meaning of Blanche's name
T. According to Eunice, it keeps on going.
U. Blanche hears this, which is not actually playing.
V. Stella is rushed there.
W. According to Stella, this is Blanche's weakness.
X. He took his own life.
Y. Lost plantation: ___ Reve

MATCHING 1 ANSWER KEY - A Streetcar Named Desire

G - 1. FIRE		A. Wedding night pajamas were made of this
U - 2. MUSIC		B. Stanley's ethnic heritage
E - 3. WOOD		C. Mitch's ____ case was from a former girlfriend.
J - 4. ILLUSION		D. New Orleans
F - 5. MITCH		E. The name DuBois means this.
D - 6. SETTING		F. He dumped Blanche when he found out about her past.
W - 7. APPEARANCE		G. The word Blanche screams
C - 8. CIGARETTE		H. Stanley threw it out the window.
B - 9. POLISH		I. Blanche said he sent a telegram.
Y -10. BELLE		J. A woman's charm is fifty percent this.
N -11. LANTERN		K. Mitch's real name
S -12. WHITE		L. Ironic apartment name; ____ Fields
T -13. LIFE		M. Author
X -14. ALLAN		N. Stanley asks Blanche if she wants to take her paper one with her.
V -15. HOSPITAL		O. He knows the gossip about Blanche.
P -16. TIARA		P. At the start of Scene 10 Blanche wears a white evening gown, slippers, and this.
M -17. WILLIAMS		Q. She ends up being sent to an institution.
K -18. HAROLD		R. Stanley buys Blanche one for her birthday.
Q -19. BLANCHE		S. Meaning of Blanche's name
R -20. TICKET		T. According to Eunice, it keeps on going.
H -21. RADIO		U. Blanche hears this, which is not actually playing.
I -22. SHEP		V. Stella is rushed there.
L -23. ELYSIAN		W. According to Stella, this is Blanche's weakness.
A -24. SILK		X. He took his own life.
O -25. SHAW		Y. Lost plantation: ____ Reve

MATCHING 2 - A Streetcar Named Desire

___ 1. ALLAN   A. A woman's charm is fifty percent this.
___ 2. TICKET   B. He knows the gossip about Blanche.
___ 3. LEAVING   C. She accuses Steve of having an affair.
___ 4. STANLEY   D. He dumped Blanche when he found out about her past.
___ 5. STREETCAR   E. Stella calls Stanley a ___.
___ 6. EUNICE   F. Stanley asks Blanche if she wants to take her paper one with her.
___ 7. LANTERN   G. It is named Desire.
___ 8. BLANCHE   H. Cheap hotel of ill repute from which Blanche was asked to leave
___ 9. LIFE   I. Blanche's destination
___10. CORN   J. Stanley buys Blanche one for her birthday.
___11. ASYLUM   K. He took his own life.
___12. MITCH   L. In Stanley's joke, the rooster stopped pursuing the hen because of this.
___13. LETTERS   M. She ends up being sent to an institution.
___14. WOOD   N. Blanche says she'll burn these that Stanley has touched.
___15. RADIO   O. Blanche renames the Flamingo The Tarantula ___ Hotel.
___16. PIG   P. Mitch's real name
___17. SHAW   Q. Stella is rushed there.
___18. FIRE   R. According to Stella, this is Blanche's weakness.
___19. RHINESTONES   S. The name DuBois means this.
___20. ILLUSION   T. False gems
___21. HAROLD   U. According to Eunice, it keeps on going.
___22. FLAMINGO   V. It would make Blanche weep with joy.
___23. ARMS   W. Stanley threw it out the window.
___24. APPEARANCE   X. He rapes Blanche.
___25. HOSPITAL   Y. The word Blanche screams

MATCHING 2 ANSWER KEY - A Streetcar Named Desire

K - 1. ALLAN		A. A woman's charm is fifty percent this.
J - 2. TICKET		B. He knows the gossip about Blanche.
V - 3. LEAVING		C. She accuses Steve of having an affair.
X - 4. STANLEY		D. He dumped Blanche when he found out about her past.
G - 5. STREETCAR		E. Stella calls Stanley a ___ .
C - 6. EUNICE		F. Stanley asks Blanche if she wants to take her paper one with her.
F - 7. LANTERN		G. It is named Desire.
M - 8. BLANCHE		H. Cheap hotel of ill repute from which Blanche was asked to leave
U - 9. LIFE		I. Blanche's destination
L -10. CORN		J. Stanley buys Blanche one for her birthday.
I -11. ASYLUM		K. He took his own life.
D -12. MITCH		L. In Stanley's joke, the rooster stopped pursuing the hen because of this.
N -13. LETTERS		M. She ends up being sent to an institution.
S -14. WOOD		N. Blanche says she'll burn these that Stanley has touched.
W 15. RADIO		O. Blanche renames the Flamingo The Tarantula ___ Hotel.
E -16. PIG		P. Mitch's real name
B -17. SHAW		Q. Stella is rushed there.
Y -18. FIRE		R. According to Stella, this is Blanche's weakness.
T -19. RHINESTONES		S. The name DuBois means this.
A -20. ILLUSION		T. False gems
P -21. HAROLD		U. According to Eunice, it keeps on going.
H -22. FLAMINGO		V. It would make Blanche weep with joy.
O -23. ARMS		W. Stanley threw it out the window.
R -24. APPEARANCE		X. He rapes Blanche.
Q -25. HOSPITAL		Y. The word Blanche screams

JUGGLE LETTERS 1 - A Streetcar Named Desire

1. PACRPEANAE = 1. _____
   According to Stella, this is Blanche's weakness.

2. GTETIECAR = 2. _____
   Mitch's ____ case was from a former girlfriend.

3. VLNIAEG = 3. _____
   It would make Blanche weep with joy.

4. GIP = 4. _____
   Stella calls Stanley a ___.

5. DDEE = 5. _____
   Proves home ownership

6. NBLHEAC = 6. _____
   She ends up being sent to an institution.

7. LITASPHO = 7. _____
   Stella is rushed there.

8. EPRKO = 8. _____
   Game Stanley and the men played

9. HAWS = 9. _____
   He knows the gossip about Blanche.

10. HULBGSITLB =10. _____
    Stanley smashed these on the wedding night.

11. GNIESTT =11. _____
    New Orleans

12. TNERRSSGA =12. _____
    Blanche depended on the kindness of ___.

13. RTIAA =13. _____
    At the start of Scene 10 Blanche wears a white evening gown, slippers, and this.

14. SNOSRNETHEI =14. _____
    False gems

15. GNNTARPE =15. _____
    Stella's condition

JUGGLE LETTERS 1 ANSWER KEY - A Streetcar Named Desire

1. PACRPEANAE = 1. APPEARANCE

   According to Stella, this is Blanche's weakness.

2. GTETIECAR = 2. CIGARETTE

   Mitch's ____ case was from a former girlfriend.

3. VLNIAEG = 3. LEAVING

   It would make Blanche weep with joy.

4. GIP = 4. PIG

   Stella calls Stanley a ___.

5. DDEE = 5. DEED

   Proves home ownership

6. NBLHEAC = 6. BLANCHE

   She ends up being sent to an institution.

7. LITASPHO = 7. HOSPITAL

   Stella is rushed there.

8. EPRKO = 8. POKER

   Game Stanley and the men played

9. HAWS = 9. SHAW

   He knows the gossip about Blanche.

10. HULBGSITLB = 10. LIGHTBULBS

    Stanley smashed these on the wedding night.

11. GNIESTT = 11. SETTING

    New Orleans

12. TNERRSSGA = 12. STRANGERS

    Blanche depended on the kindness of ___.

13. RTIAA = 13. TIARA

    At the start of Scene 10 Blanche wears a white evening gown, slippers, and this.

14. SNOSRNETHEI = 14. RHINESTONES

    False gems

15. GNNTARPE = 15. PREGNANT

    Stella's condition

JUGGLE LETTERS 2 - A Streetcar Named Desire

1. EDED = 1. _____
   Proves home ownership

2. SMUCI = 2. _____
   Blanche hears this, which is not actually playing.

3. ILLOISNU = 3. _____
   A woman's charm is fifty percent this.

4. AALLN = 4. _____
   He took his own life.

5. SUENQE = 5. _____
   Stella and Blanche are referred to as a pair of ___.

6. KTTICE = 6. _____
   Stanley buys Blanche one for her birthday.

7. ILEF = 7. _____
   According to Eunice, it keeps on going.

8. LHTPAOSI = 8. _____
   Stella is rushed there.

9. SHEITNNREOS = 9. _____
   False gems

10. CTMIH =10. _____
    He dumped Blanche when he found out about her past.

11. ILEDSPEA =11. _____
    Blanche seeks this in the sky.

12. OWDO =12. _____
    The name DuBois means this.

13. TBLEOT =13. _____
    Blanche physically threatens Stanley with a broken one.

14. CRNO =14. _____
    In Stanley's joke, the rooster stopped pursuing the hen because of this.

15. ETLSAL =15. _____
    Blanche's sister; Stanley's wife

JUGGLE LETTERS 2 ANSWER KEY - A Streetcar Named Desire

1. EDED = 1. DEED
   Proves home ownership

2. SMUCI = 2. MUSIC
   Blanche hears this, which is not actually playing.

3. ILLOISNU = 3. ILLUSION
   A woman's charm is fifty percent this.

4. AALLN = 4. ALLAN
   He took his own life.

5. SUENQE = 5. QUEENS
   Stella and Blanche are referred to as a pair of ___.

6. KTTICE = 6. TICKET
   Stanley buys Blanche one for her birthday.

7. ILEF = 7. LIFE
   According to Eunice, it keeps on going.

8. LHTPAOSI = 8. HOSPITAL
   Stella is rushed there.

9. SHEITNNREOS = 9. RHINESTONES
   False gems

10. CTMIH = 10. MITCH
    He dumped Blanche when he found out about her past.

11. ILEDSPEA = 11. PLEIADES
    Blanche seeks this in the sky.

12. OWDO = 12. WOOD
    The name DuBois means this.

13. TBLEOT = 13. BOTTLE
    Blanche physically threatens Stanley with a broken one.

14. CRNO = 14. CORN
    In Stanley's joke, the rooster stopped pursuing the hen because of this.

15. ETLSAL = 15. STELLA
    Blanche's sister; Stanley's wife

VOCABULARY RESOURCE MATERIALS

A Streetcar Named Desire Vocabulary Words

No. Word	Clue/Definition
1. AMIABILITY	Friendliness
2. ANTIQUITY	Ancient times
3. BASHFUL	Shy
4. BEAMS	Radiates
5. BELLOWING	Roaring
6. BESTIAL	Inhuman
7. CALLOUS	Insensitive
8. CLEFT	Hollowed area
9. COARSE	Natural; unprocessed
10. COMMON	Ordinary
11. COSMOPOLITAN	Worldly
12. CULTIVATED	Tended
13. DEED	Document of ownership
14. DEMURENESS	Modesty
15. DEPLETION	Scarcity
16. DESTITUTE	Without necessities; poor
17. DIFFIDENT	Timid
18. DIVESTED	Got rid of
19. DOPE	Gossip
20. EFFEMINATE	Feminine
21. ELATED	Happy
22. EXHILARATION	Feeling of stimulation
23. EXPRESSIONS	Sayings
24. EXTRACTION	Lineage; from what people one has come
25. FEIGNED	Pretended
26. GANDER	Look
27. GAUDY	Showy
28. GOSSAMER	Delicate fabric
29. GRAVELY	Seriously
30. GROTESQUE	Unnatural or ugly
31. HECTIC	Chaotic
32. HETEROGENEOUS	Different
33. HOARSELY	With a strained voice
34. HUNCHED	Bent over; crouched
35. IMMEASURABLY	Vast
36. IMPROVIDENT	Lacking judgment
37. INCONGRUOUS	Out of place
38. INDECENT	Improper
39. INDIFFERENCE	Lack of concern
40. INDISTINGUISHABLE	Not understandable; not clear
41. INDOLENT	Lazy
42. INEFFECTUAL	Unsatisfactory; not effective
43. INERT	Unable to move or act
44. INSUFFERABLY	Unbearably
45. LAPPING	Drinking up, like a dog
46. LURID	Horrible
47. MALARKEY	Foolish talk
48. MENACING	Threatening
49. NOCTURNAL	During darkness
50. NOTION	Idea

Streetcar Vocaburlary Words Continued

No.	Word	Clue/Definition
51.	OMINOUSLY	Threateningly
52.	PERPETRATED	Committed
53.	PERPETUAL	Never ending
54.	PERPLEXITY	Confusion or uncertainty
55.	PINION	Wrestle; hold down
56.	PITCH	Set talk designed to persuade
57.	PORTIERES	Heavy curtains
58.	PRIM	Stiffly proper or precise in manner or appearance
59.	PRIMITIVE	Like early mankind
60.	PRODIGIOUSLY	Wonderfully
61.	RAFFISH	Vulgar
62.	RECKON	Figure
63.	REDOLENCE	Odor; fragrance
64.	REFLECTIVELY	Thoughtfully
65.	REPERTOIRE	Collection
66.	REPROACH	Blame
67.	RETREATING	Going backwards
68.	REVERBERATED	Echoed
69.	RHUMBA	Cuban dance
70.	ROW	Fight
71.	SACCHARINE	Overly sweet
72.	SENTIMENTAL	Emotional
73.	SERENELY	Calmly
74.	SINISTER	Evil
75.	SINUOUSLY	Curving or twisting
76.	SOLEMN	Serious
77.	SPECTRAL	Ghostly
78.	SUFFICIENT	Enough
79.	SWINDLE	Scam
80.	TEMPERAMENTAL	Unpredictable; not consistent
81.	TRANQUILITY	Peace
82.	TRANSITORY	Temporary
83.	UNCAVALIER	Discourteous
84.	UNCOUTH	Crude; rough; unpolished
85.	VALISE	Suitcase
86.	VIVACITY	Liveliness
87.	VIVID	Intense
88.	VOLUPTUOUSLY	Sensuously
89.	YEARNINGLY	With desire

VOCABULARY WORD SEARCH - A Streetcar Named Desire

```
C R E P R O A C H C H B V K F Y J B E R
L D E S T I T U T E P E K I T K A D N M
E G R O T E S Q U E J S P I V S S E I J
F Y C O M M O N O B B T L S H I A H R F
T P E M D Z L W C H H I P F G B D C A K
P M F A B S E V N M U A U S M B A N H F
R E P Q R I M W U Q G L C U W L T U C N
E N R R J N N J N F R T H C L I T H C G
V A O P M I I A T L A R C O Q S N Y A W
E C D G E S R N G T V P U U N S L D S T
R I I N R T Q E G D E S I O I B D V L G
B N G I O E U L V L L T I B A N E Y Q E
E G I W W R G A U D Y S E R E N E L Y J
R H O O C S L T L V S D U E E A D R H C
A E U L N I J E J E J S P M P C M N T B
T C S L S O Q D R C A P N A R I K S Y D
E T L E U L T P C E L R D S K K N O G V
D I Y B Y R X I M W M I W S K B L I N X
W C J B S E I M O C R M Z O T B X C O B
D E T S E V I D C N F E I G N E D P V N
```

ANTIQUITY	ELATED	LURID	ROW
BASHFUL	EXPRESSIONS	MENACING	SACCHARINE
BEAMS	FEIGNED	NOTION	SERENELY
BELLOWING	GAUDY	PERPETUAL	SINISTER
BESTIAL	GOSSAMER	PINION	SOLEMN
CALLOUS	GRAVELY	PRIM	SWINDLE
CLEFT	GROTESQUE	PRODIGIOUSLY	TRANQUILITY
COMMON	HECTIC	RECKON	UNCOUTH
DEED	HUNCHED	REPROACH	VALISE
DESTITUTE	IMMEASURABLY	REVERBERATED	VIVID
DIVESTED	INERT	RHUMBA	YEARNINGLY

VOCABULARY WORD SEARCH ANSWER KEY - A Streetcar Named Desire

ANTIQUITY	ELATED	LURID	ROW
BASHFUL	EXPRESSIONS	MENACING	SACCHARINE
BEAMS	FEIGNED	NOTION	SERENELY
BELLOWING	GAUDY	PERPETUAL	SINISTER
BESTIAL	GOSSAMER	PINION	SOLEMN
CALLOUS	GRAVELY	PRIM	SWINDLE
CLEFT	GROTESQUE	PRODIGIOUSLY	TRANQUILITY
COMMON	HECTIC	RECKON	UNCOUTH
DEED	HUNCHED	REPROACH	VALISE
DESTITUTE	IMMEASURABLY	REVERBERATED	VIVID
DIVESTED	INERT	RHUMBA	YEARNINGLY

VOCABULARY CORSSWORD - A Streetcar Named Desire

Across
1. Set talk designed to persuade
3. Natural; unprocessed
5. Document of ownership
7. Inhuman
8. Tended
10. Radiates
13. Wrestle; hold down
18. Friendliness
21. Idea
22. Like early mankind
23. Fight
24. Hollowed area

Down
2. Worldly
3. Insensitive
4. Cuban dance
5. Got rid of
6. Timid
7. Roaring
9. Happy
11. Ancient times
12. Showy
14. Pretended
15. Look
16. Shy
17. Intense
19. Unable to move or act
20. Gossip

VOCABULARY CORSSWORD ANSWER KEY - A Streetcar Named Desire

Across
1. Set talk designed to persuade
3. Natural; unprocessed
5. Document of ownership
7. Inhuman
8. Tended
10. Radiates
13. Wrestle; hold down
18. Friendliness
21. Idea
22. Like early mankind
23. Fight
24. Hollowed area
Down
2. Worldly

3. Insensitive
4. Cuban dance
5. Got rid of
6. Timid
7. Roaring
9. Happy
11. Ancient times
12. Showy
14. Pretended
15. Look
16. Shy
17. Intense
19. Unable to move or act
20. Gossip

VOCABULARY MATCHING 1 - A Streetcar Named Desire

___ 1. TRANQUILITY   A. Drinking up, like a dog
___ 2. HETEROGENEOUS   B. Figure
___ 3. UNCOUTH   C. Unpredictable; not consistent
___ 4. PORTIERES   D. Happy
___ 5. DEPLETION   E. Vast
___ 6. RECKON   F. Sayings
___ 7. EXHILARATION   G. Different
___ 8. EXPRESSIONS   H. Feeling of stimulation
___ 9. IMMEASURABLY   I. Going backwards
___10. ROW   J. Crude; rough; unpolished
___11. YEARNINGLY   K. Evil
___12. ELATED   L. Fight
___13. SUFFICIENT   M. Out of place
___14. SINISTER   N. With desire
___15. TEMPERAMENTAL   O. Enough
___16. INDOLENT   P. Lazy
___17. AMIABILITY   Q. Ordinary
___18. VIVACITY   R. Unnatural or ugly
___19. PRIM   S. Heavy curtains
___20. GROTESQUE   T. Peace
___21. INCONGRUOUS   U. Stiffly proper or precise in manner or appearance
___22. COMMON   V. Scarcity
___23. RETREATING   W. Radiates
___24. BEAMS   X. Friendliness
___25. LAPPING   Y. Liveliness

VOCABULARY MATCHING 1 ANSWER KEY - A Streetcar Named Desire

T - 1. TRANQUILITY		A. Drinking up, like a dog
G - 2. HETEROGENEOUS		B. Figure
J - 3. UNCOUTH		C. Unpredictable; not consistent
S - 4. PORTIERES		D. Happy
V - 5. DEPLETION		E. Vast
B - 6. RECKON		F. Sayings
H - 7. EXHILARATION		G. Different
F - 8. EXPRESSIONS		H. Feeling of stimulation
E - 9. IMMEASURABLY		I. Going backwards
L - 10. ROW		J. Crude; rough; unpolished
N - 11. YEARNINGLY		K. Evil
D - 12. ELATED		L. Fight
O - 13. SUFFICIENT		M. Out of place
K - 14. SINISTER		N. With desire
C - 15. TEMPERAMENTAL		O. Enough
P - 16. INDOLENT		P. Lazy
X - 17. AMIABILITY		Q. Ordinary
Y - 18. VIVACITY		R. Unnatural or ugly
U - 19. PRIM		S. Heavy curtains
R - 20. GROTESQUE		T. Peace
M - 21. INCONGRUOUS		U. Stiffly proper or precise in manner or appearance
Q - 22. COMMON		V. Scarcity
I - 23. RETREATING		W. Radiates
W - 24. BEAMS		X. Friendliness
A - 25. LAPPING		Y. Liveliness

VOCABULARY MATCHING 2 - A Streetcar Named Desire

___ 1. PRIMITIVE   A. Fight
___ 2. HECTIC   B. Friendliness
___ 3. PINION   C. Delicate fabric
___ 4. AMIABILITY   D. Serious
___ 5. LAPPING   E. Lazy
___ 6. PERPETUAL   F. Calmly
___ 7. SUFFICIENT   G. Horrible
___ 8. SENTIMENTAL   H. Emotional
___ 9. SOLEMN   I. Committed
___10. DEED   J. Wrestle; hold down
___11. COMMON   K. Never ending
___12. LURID   L. With a strained voice
___13. REPERTOIRE   M. Like early mankind
___14. SERENELY   N. Foolish talk
___15. EFFEMINATE   O. Collection
___16. REDOLENCE   P. Feminine
___17. ANTIQUITY   Q. Chaotic
___18. INERT   R. Ancient times
___19. ROW   S. Unable to move or act
___20. INDOLENT   T. Document of ownership
___21. GOSSAMER   U. Ordinary
___22. MALARKEY   V. Drinking up, like a dog
___23. PERPETRATED   W. Odor; fragrance
___24. HOARSELY   X. Discourteous
___25. UNCAVALIER   Y. Enough

VOCABULARY MATCHING 2 ANSWER KEY - A Streetcar Named Desire

M - 1. PRIMITIVE   A. Fight

Q - 2. HECTIC   B. Friendliness

J - 3. PINION   C. Delicate fabric

B - 4. AMIABILITY   D. Serious

V - 5. LAPPING   E. Lazy

K - 6. PERPETUAL   F. Calmly

Y - 7. SUFFICIENT   G. Horrible

H - 8. SENTIMENTAL   H. Emotional

D - 9. SOLEMN   I. Committed

T - 10. DEED   J. Wrestle; hold down

U - 11. COMMON   K. Never ending

G - 12. LURID   L. With a strained voice

O - 13. REPERTOIRE   M. Like early mankind

F - 14. SERENELY   N. Foolish talk

P - 15. EFFEMINATE   O. Collection

W - 16. REDOLENCE   P. Feminine

R - 17. ANTIQUITY   Q. Chaotic

S - 18. INERT   R. Ancient times

A - 19. ROW   S. Unable to move or act

E - 20. INDOLENT   T. Document of ownership

C - 21. GOSSAMER   U. Ordinary

N - 22. MALARKEY   V. Drinking up, like a dog

I - 23. PERPETRATED   W. Odor; fragrance

L - 24. HOARSELY   X. Discourteous

X - 25. UNCAVALIER   Y. Enough

VOCABULARY JUGGLE LETTERS 1 - A Streetcar Named Desire

1. INOSLUYUS = 1. _____
   Curving or twisting

2. ETARNGIETR = 2. _____
   Going backwards

3. SUOUUVOLLTPY = 3. _____
   Sensuously

4. FFAMEIETNE = 4. _____
   Feminine

5. WEIDNSL = 5. _____
   Scam

6. SVDDEIET = 6. _____
   Got rid of

7. EDED = 7. _____
   Document of ownership

8. IMVPERTII = 8. _____
   Like early mankind

9. AUGDY = 9. _____
   Showy

10. VDIIV = 10. _____
    Intense

11. OLEDENREC = 11. _____
    Odor; fragrance

12. SUYOPRLIGIOD = 12. _____
    Wonderfully

13. VEREABRREEDT = 13. _____
    Echoed

14. UUGSCNIRONO = 14. _____
    Out of place

VOCABULARY JUGGLE LETTERS 1 ANSWER KEY - A Streetcar Named Desire

1. INOSLUYUS = 1. SINUOUSLY
   Curving or twisting

2. ETARNGIETR = 2. RETREATING
   Going backwards

3. SUOUUVOLLTPY = 3. VOLUPTUOUSLY
   Sensuously

4. FFAMEIETNE = 4. EFFEMINATE
   Feminine

5. WEIDNSL = 5. SWINDLE
   Scam

6. SVDDEIET = 6. DIVESTED
   Got rid of

7. EDED = 7. DEED
   Document of ownership

8. IMVPERTII = 8. PRIMITIVE
   Like early mankind

9. AUGDY = 9. GAUDY
   Showy

10. VDIIV = 10. VIVID
    Intense

11. OLEDENREC = 11. REDOLENCE
    Odor; fragrance

12. SUYOPRLIGIOD = 12. PRODIGIOUSLY
    Wonderfully

13. VEREABRREEDT = 13. REVERBERATED
    Echoed

14. UUGSCNIRONO = 14. INCONGRUOUS
    Out of place

VOCABULARY JUGGLE LETTTERS 2 - A Streetcar Named Desire

1. NTIEIRSS = 1. _____
   Evil

2. FEEIRVYLELTC = 2. _____
   Thoughtfully

3. NIETR = 3. _____
   Unable to move or act

4. OPINNI = 4. _____
   Wrestle; hold down

5. TLAEED = 5. _____
   Happy

6. DGIFEEN = 6. _____
   Pretended

7. TEIRGRTAEN = 7. _____
   Going backwards

8. AGDUY = 8. _____
   Showy

9. GSONTEOEEERHU = 9. _____
   Different

10. IYQTLUARNIT =10. _____
    Peace

11. OMSGERAS =11. _____
    Delicate fabric

12. LSIYSUONU =12. _____
    Curving or twisting

13. UTSUPLYLVOUO =13. _____
    Sensuously

14. LOLSACU =14. _____
    Insensitive

VOCABULARY JUGGLE LETTTERS 2 ANSWER KEY - A Streetcar Named Desire

1. NTIEIRSS = 1. SINISTER
Evil

2. FEEIRVYLELTC = 2. REFLECTIVELY
Thoughtfully

3. NIETR = 3. INERT
Unable to move or act

4. OPINNI = 4. PINION
Wrestle; hold down

5. TLAEED = 5. ELATED
Happy

6. DGIFEEN = 6. FEIGNED
Pretended

7. TEIRGRTAEN = 7. RETREATING
Going backwards

8. AGDUY = 8. GAUDY
Showy

9. GSONTEOEEERHU = 9. HETEROGENEOUS
Different

10. IYQTLUARNIT = 10. TRANQUILITY
Peace

11. OMSGERAS = 11. GOSSAMER
Delicate fabric

12. LSIYSUONU = 12. SINUOUSLY
Curving or twisting

13. UTSUPLYLVOUO = 13. VOLUPTUOUSLY
Sensuously

14. LOLSACU = 14. CALLOUS
Insensitive

www.ingramcontent.com/pod-product-compliance
Lightning Source LLC
Chambersburg PA
CBHW051406070526
44584CB00023B/3315